First World War
and Army of Occupation
War Diary
France, Belgium and Germany

2 CAVALRY DIVISION
Divisional Troops
2 Field Squadron Royal Engineers
4 August 1914 - 30 April 1919

WO95/1123/6

The Naval & Military Press Ltd
www.nmarchive.com
Published in association with The National Archives

Published by

The Naval & Military Press Ltd

Unit 10 Ridgewood Industrial Park,

Uckfield, East Sussex,

TN22 5QE England

Tel: +44 (0) 1825 749494

www.naval-military-press.com

www.nmarchive.com

This diary has been reprinted in facsimile from the original. Any imperfections are inevitably reproduced and the quality may fall short of modern type and cartographic standards.

© **Crown Copyright**
Images reproduced by permission of The National Archives, London, England, 2015.

Contents

Document type	Place/Title	Date From	Date To
Heading	WO95/1123/3		
Heading	1914-1919 2nd Cavalry Division 2nd Field Squadn R.E. Aug 1914-Aug 1919		
Heading	Field Troops R.E. August 1914. Aug 1919		
Miscellaneous	A Form. Messages And Signals.		
War Diary		04/08/1914	31/08/1914
Heading	Field Troop R.E. September 1914		
War Diary		02/09/1914	30/09/1914
Heading	2nd Cavalry Divisional Engineers Disembarked Havre 11.10.14. 2nd Field Squadron R.E. October 1914		
War Diary	Taux	01/10/1914	31/10/1914
Heading	2nd Cavalry Divisional Engineers 2nd Field Squadron R.E. November 1914		
War Diary		01/11/1914	30/11/1914
Heading	2nd Cavalry Divisional Engineers 2nd Field Squadron R.E. December 1914		
War Diary		01/12/1914	31/12/1914
War Diary		23/12/1914	23/12/1914
Heading	2nd Cavalry Division 2nd Field Squadron R.E. Vol VI 1-1.1.15		
War Diary		01/01/1915	31/01/1915
Heading	2nd Cavalry Division 2nd Field Squadron R.E. Vol VII 1-28.2.15		
War Diary		01/02/1915	23/02/1915
War Diary		21/02/1915	28/02/1915
Heading	2nd Field Squadron R.E. Vol VIII 1-31.3.15. 2nd Cavalry Division		
War Diary		01/03/1915	08/03/1915
War Diary		04/03/1915	22/03/1915
War Diary		10/03/1915	13/03/1915
War Diary		12/03/1915	23/03/1915
War Diary		22/03/1915	25/03/1915
War Diary		01/03/1915	08/03/1915
War Diary		04/03/1915	22/03/1915
War Diary		10/03/1915	13/03/1915
War Diary		12/03/1915	20/03/1915
War Diary		19/03/1915	31/03/1915
War Diary		22/03/1915	25/03/1915
War Diary		26/03/1915	31/03/1915
War Diary		30/03/1915	30/03/1915
Heading	2nd Cavalry Division 2nd Field Squadron R.E. Vol IX 3-30.4.15		
War Diary		03/04/1915	22/04/1915
War Diary		17/04/1915	30/04/1915
Heading	2nd Cavalry Division 2nd Field Squadron R.E. Vol X 1-31.5.15		
War Diary		01/05/1915	31/05/1915
Heading	2nd Cavalry Division 2nd Field Squadron R.E. Vol XI June To July 1915		
War Diary		01/06/1915	31/07/1915

War Diary		01/07/1915	18/07/1915
War Diary		19/07/1915	31/07/1915
War Diary		24/07/1915	24/07/1915
Heading	2nd Cavalry Division 2nd Field Squadron R.E. Vol XII August 1.15		
War Diary		00/08/1915	00/08/1915
War Diary		06/08/1915	06/08/1915
Heading	2nd Cavalry Division 2nd Field Squadron R.E. Vol XIII Sept 1.15		
War Diary		01/09/1915	30/09/1915
Heading	O.C. 2nd Fd. Cs. R.E. Oct 1915 Vol XI		
War Diary		02/10/1915	30/10/1915
Heading	8th Division 2nd Fd Sqr. R.E. Nov 1915 Vol XII		
War Diary		01/10/1915	30/10/1915
War Diary		29/10/1915	29/10/1915
Heading	No. 2. Fd. Sqr. R.E. Dec 1915 Vol XVI		
War Diary	Le Nieppe	01/12/1915	31/12/1915
War Diary	Willametz	01/01/1916	31/01/1916
War Diary	Willametz	01/02/1916	29/02/1916
War Diary	Willametz	01/03/1916	31/03/1916
War Diary	Willametz	01/04/1916	12/05/1916
War Diary	Ledinghem	14/05/1916	30/06/1916
Heading	War Diary of 2nd Field Squadron. R.E. from: 1st July to: 31st July. 1916. (Volume XXIII).		
War Diary	Au Souverain	01/07/1916	31/07/1916
Heading	War Diary of 2nd Field Squadron R.E. for August, 1916. Vol		
War Diary		01/08/1916	31/08/1916
Heading	War Diary of 2nd Field Squadron, R.E. for September, 1916. Volume		
War Diary		01/09/1916	26/09/1916
Heading	War Diary of 2nd Field Squadron, R.E. October, 1916 Vol. 25		
War Diary	Fricourt	01/10/1916	14/10/1916
War Diary	Fricourt	01/10/1916	31/10/1916
Heading	War Diary of 2nd Field Squadron, R.E. November, 1916 Vol 26		
War Diary	Fricourt	01/10/1916	26/10/1916
War Diary	Fricourt	12/10/1916	26/10/1916
Heading	War Diary of 2nd Field Squadron, R.E. December, 1916. Vol. 27		
War Diary		01/12/1916	14/12/1916
Heading	War Diary of 2nd Field Squadron, R.E. January, 1917 Vol. XXIX.		
War Diary	Ponches Estruval	01/01/1917	15/01/1917
War Diary	Ponches Estruval	02/01/1917	25/01/1917
War Diary	Ponches Estruval	08/01/1917	29/01/1917
Heading	War Diary of 2nd Field Squadron, R.E. February, 1917. Vol. XXX.		
War Diary	Ponches-Estruval	01/02/1917	19/02/1917
War Diary	Ponches-Estruval	02/02/1917	28/02/1917
War Diary	Ponches-Estruval	05/02/1917	25/02/1917
Heading	War Diary of 2nd Field Squadron, R.E. March, 1917. Vol XXXI.		
War Diary	Ponches	13/03/1917	15/03/1917
War Diary	Ponches	03/03/1917	19/03/1917

War Diary	Ponches	08/03/1917	31/03/1917
War Diary	Ponches	30/03/1917	31/03/1917
Heading	War Diary of 2nd Field Squadron, R.E. April, 1917. Vol. XXXII.		
War Diary	Ponches-Estruval	01/04/1917	11/04/1917
War Diary	Agny	12/04/1917	12/04/1917
War Diary	Henu	13/04/1917	30/04/1917
War Diary	Henu	21/04/1917	21/04/1917
Heading	War Diary of 2nd Field Squadron, R.E. From 1.5.17 to 31.5.17. Volume XXXII		
War Diary	Henu	01/05/1917	31/05/1917
War Diary	Henu	25/05/1917	31/05/1917
War Diary	Henu	24/05/1917	24/05/1917
Heading	War Diary of 2nd Field Squadron, R.E. From 1.6.17 To 30.6.17 (Volume 34)		
War Diary	Roisel	01/06/1917	29/06/1917
War Diary	Roisel	01/06/1917	30/06/1917
War Diary	Roisel	04/06/1917	04/06/1917
Heading	War Diary of 2nd Field Squadron, R.E. From 1.7.17 To 31.7.17 (Volume 35)		
War Diary	Roisel	01/07/1917	06/07/1917
War Diary	Roisel	03/07/1917	06/07/1917
War Diary	Marquaix	06/07/1917	16/07/1917
War Diary	Magnicourt	17/07/1917	31/07/1917
Heading	War Diary of 2nd Field Squadron, R.E. From 1.8.17 to 31.8.17 (Volume-36)		
War Diary	Magnicourt Sur Cansur	01/08/1917	31/08/1917
War Diary	Magnicourt Sur Cansur	14/08/1917	14/08/1917
Heading	War Diary of 2nd Field Squadron, R.E. From 1.9.17 To 30.9.17 Volume No. 37		
War Diary	Magnicourt.	01/09/1917	24/09/1917
Heading	War Diary of 2nd Field Squadron, R.E. From 1.10.17 to 31.10.17 Volume Number No 38		
War Diary		01/10/1917	31/10/1917
War Diary		24/10/1917	31/10/1917
Heading	War Diary of 2nd Field Squadron, R.E. From 1.11.17 to 30.11.17 Volume No. 39		
War Diary	Brusle	01/11/1917	24/11/1917
War Diary	Dessart Wood	25/11/1917	30/11/1917
Heading	War Diary of 2nd Field Squadron, R.E. From 1.12.17 to 31.12.17 Vol XL		
War Diary	Dessart Wood (Fins)	01/12/1917	08/12/1917
War Diary	Nampty	09/12/1917	19/12/1917
War Diary	Hervilly	21/12/1917	31/12/1917
Heading	War Diary of 2nd Field Squadron, R.E. from 1.1.18 to 31.1.18 Volume No. 41		
War Diary	Hervilly	01/01/1918	22/01/1918
War Diary	Hervilly	18/01/1918	27/01/1918
War Diary	Hervilly	23/01/1918	31/01/1918
War Diary	Hervilly	13/01/1918	16/01/1918
War Diary	Hervilly	06/01/1918	06/01/1918
Heading	War Diary of 2nd Field Squadron, R.E. From 1.2.18 to 28.2.18 Volume No. 42		
War Diary	Hervilly	01/02/1918	13/02/1918
War Diary	Hervilly	07/02/1918	08/02/1918
War Diary	Fourgules	14/02/1918	16/02/1918

War Diary	Fourgules	09/02/1918	28/02/1918
War Diary	Fourques	01/03/1918	07/03/1918
War Diary	Vermand	01/03/1918	11/03/1918
War Diary	Vermand	10/03/1918	10/03/1918
War Diary	Fourques	11/03/1918	13/03/1918
War Diary	Maucourt	13/03/1918	22/03/1918
War Diary	Maucourt	21/03/1918	22/03/1918
War Diary	Pomtoise	23/03/1918	23/03/1918
War Diary	Bailly	24/03/1918	27/03/1918
War Diary	Bailly	26/03/1918	26/03/1918
War Diary	Jonquieres	27/03/1918	27/03/1918
War Diary	Ausauvillers	28/03/1918	29/03/1918
War Diary	Boves	29/03/1918	31/03/1918
Heading	War Diary of 2nd Field Squadron R.E. From 1.4.18 to 30.4.18 Volume No. 44		
War Diary	Boves	01/04/1918	02/04/1918
War Diary	Rivery	03/04/1918	04/04/1918
War Diary	Famechon	06/04/1918	09/04/1918
War Diary	Auxi Le Chateau	10/04/1918	10/04/1918
War Diary	Petigny	12/04/1918	12/04/1918
War Diary	Blaringhem	13/04/1918	21/04/1918
War Diary	Coyecque	29/04/1918	29/04/1918
War Diary	Coyecque	19/04/1918	25/04/1918
Heading	War Diary of 2nd Field Squadron R.E. From 1/5/18 to 3/5/18 Volume No. 45		
War Diary	Coyecque	01/05/1918	01/05/1918
War Diary	Le Marais	02/05/1918	04/05/1918
War Diary	Alette	05/04/1918	19/04/1918
War Diary	Froidval	20/04/1918	20/04/1918
War Diary	Vielfort	21/05/1918	31/05/1918
Heading	War Diary of 2nd Field Squadron R.E. from 1/6/18 to 30/6/18 Volume No. 46		
War Diary	Vielfort	01/06/1918	30/06/1918
War Diary	Cayeux	17/05/1918	30/05/1918
War Diary	Cayeux	17/05/1918	17/05/1918
Heading	War Diary of 2nd Field Squadron R.E. From 1.7.18 To 31.7.18 Volume No. 47		
War Diary	Vielfort (near Houdain)	01/07/1918	10/07/1918
War Diary		10/07/1918	10/07/1918
War Diary	Willencourt (Vielfort)	11/07/1918	11/07/1918
War Diary	Willencourt (Vielfort)	09/07/1918	09/07/1918
War Diary	Willencourt	12/07/1918	13/07/1918
War Diary	Sars-Lez-Bois	15/07/1918	16/07/1918
War Diary	Willencourt	22/07/1918	31/07/1918
War Diary	Willencourt	26/07/1918	26/07/1918
Heading	War Diary of 2nd Field Squadron R.E. from 1.8.18 to 31.8.18 Volume No. 48		
War Diary	Willencourt	01/08/1918	05/08/1918
War Diary	Hanchy	05/08/1918	06/08/1918
War Diary	Breilly	06/07/1918	07/07/1918
War Diary	Longeau	07/07/1918	08/07/1918
War Diary	Caix	08/07/1918	08/07/1918
War Diary	Warvillers.	09/07/1918	09/07/1918
War Diary	Vrely	10/07/1918	11/07/1918
War Diary	Aubercourt	11/07/1918	14/07/1918
War Diary	Belloy-Sur-Somme.	15/07/1918	15/07/1918

War Diary	Canaples	16/07/1918	18/07/1918
War Diary	Caumont	18/07/1918	22/07/1918
War Diary	Grenas	22/07/1918	22/07/1918
War Diary	Bailleulval (Ayette)	23/07/1918	23/07/1918
War Diary	Bailleulval	24/07/1918	24/07/1918
War Diary	Grenas	24/07/1918	24/07/1918
War Diary	Miraumont	25/07/1918	31/07/1918
Heading	War Diary of 2nd Field Squadron R.E. From 1.9.18 to 30.9.18 Volume No. 49		
War Diary	Mirau Mont	01/09/1918	03/09/1918
War Diary	Famechon	03/09/1918	17/09/1918
War Diary	Famechon	06/09/1918	17/09/1918
War Diary	Goadiempre	17/09/1918	30/09/1918
War Diary	Goadiempre	28/09/1918	28/09/1918
War Diary	Goadiempre	26/09/1918	29/09/1918
Heading	War Diary of 2nd Field Squadron R.E. from 1.10.18 To 31.10.18 Volume No. 50		
War Diary	Guadienpre	01/10/1918	31/10/1918
War Diary	Guadienpre	21/10/1918	21/10/1918
War Diary	Guadienpre	16/10/1918	29/10/1918
War Diary	Guadienpre	01/10/1918	31/10/1918
War Diary	Guadienpre	03/10/1918	10/10/1918
War Diary	Guadienpre	01/10/1918	31/10/1918
Heading	War Diary November 1918 Volume No. 51		
War Diary	Guadiemore Badauale	01/11/1918	05/11/1918
War Diary	Cambrai	06/11/1918	06/11/1918
War Diary	Cambrai	05/11/1918	13/11/1918
War Diary	Cambrai	12/11/1918	12/11/1918
War Diary	Boussies	13/11/1918	13/11/1918
War Diary	Hugemont Champ	13/11/1918	14/11/1918
War Diary	Maubeuge	15/11/1918	16/11/1918
War Diary	Lobbes	17/11/1918	17/11/1918
War Diary	Hanzimelle	18/11/1918	21/11/1918
War Diary	Dinant	21/11/1918	21/11/1918
War Diary	Chapois	22/11/1918	22/11/1918
War Diary	Jamodine	23/11/1918	29/11/1918
War Diary	Jamodine	29/11/1918	29/11/1918
War Diary	Marloie	29/11/1918	30/11/1918
War Diary	Marloie	10/11/1918	10/11/1918
Heading	War Diary of 2nd Field Squadron R.E. Volume No. 52 From 1.12.18 To 31.12.18		
War Diary	Marloie	01/12/1918	15/12/1918
War Diary	12 Ier	16/12/1918	16/12/1918
War Diary	Tilff	17/12/1918	20/12/1918
War Diary	Tilff	17/12/1918	31/12/1918
War Diary	Tilff	09/12/1918	09/12/1918
Heading	War Diary of 2nd Field Squadron R.E. from 1.1.19 to 31.1.19 Volume No. 53		
War Diary	Tilff	01/01/1919	31/01/1919
War Diary	Theux	01/01/1919	31/01/1919
Heading	War Diary of 2nd Field Squadron R.E. Volume No. 54. from 1.2.19 to 28.2.19		
War Diary	Tilff	01/02/1919	18/02/1919
War Diary	Tilff	17/02/1919	28/02/1919
Heading	War Diary of 2nd Field Squadron R.E. Volume No. 55. March 1919		

War Diary	Tilff	01/03/1919	08/03/1919
War Diary	Tilff	07/03/1919	07/03/1919
War Diary	Ensival	10/03/1916	31/03/1916
Heading	War Diary of 2nd Field Squadron R.E. Volume No. 57 April 1919		
War Diary	Ensival	12/04/1919	30/04/1919

Do 95/11/23/3

1914-1919
2ND CAVALRY DIVISION

2ND FIELD SQUADN R.E.

AUG 1914-APL 1919

FIELD TROOPS R. E.

AUGUST 1914.

Apl 1919

"A" Form.   Army Form C. 2121.
MESSAGES AND SIGNALS.   No. of Message_____

Prefix	Code	m.	Words	Charge	This message is on a/c of:	Recd. at _____ m.
Office of Origin and Service Instructions.			Sent			Date _____
			At _____ m.		_____ Service.	From _____
			To _____			
			By _____		(Signature of "Franking Officer.")	By _____

TO { CHAUNY Light Railway Bridge destroyed
     by 3° To RE

| Sender's Number | Day of Month | In reply to Number | A A A |

Light Ry Bridge 1 m. E of Chauny
main Girders as before with two light
girders under rails
Placed 12 lb charges as before on top &
bottom flanges 3 lb at cross brace junction
& 1½ lb on small girders.
     Total 74 lb.

From   Result Bridge cut clean & dropped
Place into canal.
Time

The above may be forwarded as now corrected.   (Z)
_____   _____
       Censor.   Signature of Addressor or person authorised to telegraph in his name.
          * This line should be erased if not required.

"A" Form. Army Form C. 212
MESSAGES AND SIGNALS. No. of Message_____

Prefix___ Code___ m.	Words	Charge	This message is on a/c of:	Recd. at___ m.
Office of Origin and Service Instructions.	Sent			Date___
	At___ m.		___Service.	From___
	To___			By___
	By___		(Signature of "Franking Officer.")	

TO — CHAUNY Road Bridge Prepared for demn

Sender's Number | Day of Month | In reply to Number | **A A A**

Chauny

2 main girders as shown. Roadway supported on cross girders & brick Jack Arches.

Span about 70'
both ——— 24'

Angles 4"×4"
Cross braces
Rivets ½"

$C = \frac{3}{2} B t^2$

Web $= \frac{3}{2} × \frac{3}{2} × \frac{1}{4} = \frac{1}{2}$ lb
flange $\frac{3}{2} × \frac{2}{3} × \frac{1}{4} = \frac{1}{4}$
Angles $\frac{3}{2} × \frac{1}{2} × \frac{25}{4} = 3$ lb
$\frac{3}{2} × \frac{2}{3} × 4 = 4$

$7\frac{3}{4}$ lb

Allow 12 lb on each top & bottom flange + 3 lb where cross braces meet. Placed as in M.F.E.

Total 52 lb.

hot demolished

From___
Place___
Time___

The above may be forwarded as now corrected. (Z) Charge reversed to order

Censor.   Signature of Addressor or person authorised to telegraph in his name.

* This line should be erased if not required.

Army Form C. 2118.

WAR DIARY
or
INTELLIGENCE SUMMARY
(Erase heading not required.)

Instructions regarding War Diaries and Intelligence Summaries are contained in F. S. Regs., Part II. and the Staff Manual respectively. Title pages will be prepared in manuscript.

Hour, Date, Place	Summary of Events and Information	Remarks and references to Appendices
4. 8. 14	1st day of mobilization	
11- 8. 14	Mobilization reported complete. Entrained Curragh Siding 8 A.M. Arrived at Queenstown 3. P.M.	
15- 8. 14	Left Queenstown in S.S. Rossa 6 P.M.	
16. 8. 14	At sea.	
17- 8. 14	Arrived Havre :- Landed 6 A.M. Cancelled oil :-	
18. 8. 14	Stayed at No. 2. Camp Havre. Entrained 11-15 P.M. for	
19- 8. 14	BOBIGNY & then AULNOYE where arrived 11-0 P.M.	
20. 8. 14	Lype AULNOYE for BOUSSIERE 8 A.M. arrived 9-30 A.M. Sent report to Base Commandant Havre re. Mjr Price & Pte. Salmon Kilrane, who should otherwise at HAVRE & have not yet rejoined	

Army Form C. 2118.

WAR DIARY
or
INTELLIGENCE SUMMARY
(Erase heading not required.)

Instructions regarding War Diaries and Intelligence Summaries are contained in F. S. Regs., Part II. and the Staff Manual respectively. Title pages will be prepared in manuscript.

Hour, Date, Place	Summary of Events and Information	Remarks and references to Appendices
23-8-14	Left Sugar Factory 4 A.M. Sunday all vehicles touch. Received gun-fire Regiments. Full up Transport. Waited for G.O.C. went with R.E. Troop & came under shrapnel fire 9-11 A.M. No casualties. K.S. & J. BONNET. Returned to Billets at HARGNIES.	
25-8-14	Left HARGNIES 1 P.M. & TAISNIERES Billeted 12 M.N.	
26-8-14	Left TAISNIERES with Transport at 4-30 A.M. reached HANAPPE. X killed 2 P.M.	
27-8-14	Marched to MARQUIGNY and billeted.	
28-8-14	Marched to SINCENY near LA FÈRE and CHAUNY.	
29-8-14	Placed charges on road & railway bridges over OISE CANAL at CHAUNY. 3 P.M. 30-8-14	
30- " "	Destroyed railway bridge. Blowing away but effectually destroyed showing enemy prepared, Retired to ST GOBAIN & SANDRY 25 miles.	
31-8-14	Marched to DONMIERS left at midnight for CONDE LRS:—	

French Aylof 1st MR
late O.C. Field Troop R.E.

FIELD TROOP   R. E.

SEPTEMBER 1914.

Army Form C. 2118.

WAR DIARY
or
INTELLIGENCE SUMMARY.
(Erase heading not required.)

Field Troop R.E. 5th Cav. Bde. & 2 Cav. Div:

Hour, Date, Place	Summary of Events and Information	Remarks and references to Appendices
2/9/14	Left MISSY 5pm for TRIPORT. Billets. Braine via road. R.½ Troop to S.JEAN for Field Bridge over MARNE. Commenced preparing for demolition. Work completed by 10 pm. Remainder as Billet.	
3/9/14	Left for Rd at PEZON 3 am arrived 7 pm. Bivouacked.	
4/9/14	RESTED as BILLET (LAGNY-sur-MARNE) Dawn arrived 7 am. left 2 pm	
5/9/14	BIVOUAC arrived 3 am. left 2 pm for BERNAY bivouacked 7 pm	
6/9/14	Left for LUMIGNY 1 am. Rdvous 2 Troop cart with Bde Commander Transport Bivouacked. Patrol from front turned North here.	
7/9/14	Left for REBAIS 8 am. Billet 7 pm	
8/9/14	8 am. Action at GIBRALTAR Bivouacked at BOITRON. Pat from Troop.	
9/9/14	8 am. Pat from Troop at holding Lock bivouacked 8 pm CHARLY	
10/9/14	5 am. Patrol 9–3 pm C. MARIGNY bivouacked 7 pm CHEZY & ORXOIS	
11/9/14	6 am from CHARTEUVES billet 4 am. + wet	
12/9/14	6-30 am arrived GERY 5 pm billet 9 pm	
13/9/14		
14/9/14	10 am. Bivouacked 7 pm to Lat	
14.9.14 6	6-30 am fr CHASSEMY billet CERSEUIL 9 o.f.m. CERSEUIL. Strengthen Cav. outposts before CONDÉ. Improve water supply in BRAINE.	
15.9.14 to	7 Raff wagons, 14 Lim 23 horses from Regt of 2 Cav. Bde. 4.9 this joined. Troop reduced to receiving 2 Jr/sgrs, 1st & 3rd Squadron. + 2 boat wagons so as to act as 2 Cav. Div: Engineers. Troop becomes a Divisional Unit.	
26.9.14	Lce Troop under Lt. R.G. STONE joined from 1st Squadron, 1 O. 33 hr & 32 horses 3 Vehicles & Bicycles. 1 Reinforcements (9 Men) + 16 Reservists arrived. Boat wagon arrives.	
27 & 29.9.14	Remain at CERSEUIL. 30.9.14 March to TAUX	

J.C. Trench Capt R.E.

2nd Cavalry Divisional Engineers

Disembarked Havre 11.10.14.

2nd FIELD SQUADRON R. E.

OCTOBER 1914.

Army Form C. 2118.

WAR DIARY
or
INTELLIGENCE SUMMARY.

9th Field Squadron RE   p 1

(Erase heading not required.)

Instructions regarding War Diaries and Intelligence Summaries are contained in F.S. Regs., Part II. and the Staff Manual respectively. Title pages will be prepared in manuscript.

Hour, Date, Place	Summary of Events and Information	Remarks and references to Appendices
TAUX Oct. 1st 1914	Remained at TAUX	
— 2	Marched to FLEURY	
— 3	ST VAAST	
— 4	LE PLOYRON	
— 6	THENNES	
— 6	Remained at ST VAAST	
— 7	Marched to ST VAAST	
—	CONTEVILLE	
— 8	BERMICOURT	
— 9	FONTES	
— 10	LILETTE	
— 11		
— 12	CAESTRE	
	On the 19th Oct. 1914 the 2nd Field Squadron R.E. embarked at Southampton, arriving at LE HAVRE on the 11th & reached HAZEBROUCK by train on the 14th, billetting at CAESTRE	
— 13	GODEWAERSWELDE	
— 14	WESTOUTRE	
— 15	WESTOUTRE where the English portion joined up with & absorbed the old 9th Field Troop R.E.	

Army Form C. 2118.

2

3rd Field Squadron R.E.

WAR DIARY
or
INTELLIGENCE SUMMARY.
(Erase heading not required.)

Instructions regarding War Diaries and Intelligence Summaries are contained in F.S. Regs., Part II. and the Staff Manual respectively. Title pages will be prepared in manuscript.

Hour, Date, Place	Summary of Events and Information	Remarks and references to Appendices
16.10.14	To WYTSCHAETE. Strengthening outpost position for Cavalry	
17.10.14	at WYTSCHAETE " "	
18.10.14	To MESSINES. HOUTHEM & GAPAARD - back to	
19.10.14	WYTSCHAETE. Remained at WYTSCHAETE helping in strengthening line held by 2nd Cav. Bn. from HOUTTEM to GAPAARD	
20.10.14	as for 19th	
21.10.14	Begun defence works on 2nd line from St ELOI to WYTSCHAETE	
22.10.14	Billeted at OOSTTAVERNE work as before & nightwork in helping Strengthen Cavalry lines.	
23.10.14	As for 22nd	
24.10.14	— 23rd	
25.10.14	— 24th	
26.10.14	Billets at GROOTE VIERSTRAAT. work as before.	
27.10.14	as for 26th	

Army Form C. 2118.

WAR DIARY
or
INTELLIGENCE SUMMARY.
(Erase heading not required.)

Hour, Date, Place	Summary of Events and Information	Remarks and references to Appendices
28.10.14.	Billets at GROOTE VIERSTADT took as before on the Cavalry lines, blk preparing and points & holding on part line at night	
29.10.14.	As for 28th	
30.10.14	On this day the Cavalry were pushed back from their front line & fell back to the line previously prepared thro' (ST ELOI & WYTSCHAETE KMESSINES) Bnd Wks to hand to LA CAYTTE, sending a troop and to help to hold on their line	
31.10.14.		E.O. Johnson Capt. RE O.C. 2nd Field Squadron RE

2nd Cavalry Divisional Engineers

───────────

2nd FIELD SQUADRON R. E.

NOVEMBER 1914.

Army Form C. 2118.

WAR DIARY
or
INTELLIGENCE SUMMARY.
(Erase heading not required.)

Instructions regarding War Diaries and Intelligence Summaries are contained in F.S. Regs., Part II. and the Staff Manual respectively. Title pages will be prepared in manuscript.

Hour, Date, Place	Summary of Events and Information	Remarks and references to Appendices
1–11–14	3 Troops went out to help 2nd & 5th Sqns on outpost line but	
2–11–14	P BAPAUME TRENCHES? March strong. Changed billets to REININGHELST.	
3–11–14.	Changed billets to farm 2 miles N of BAILLEUL. 3 Troops sent out at night to help STABLE with bivouac on the line. ½ mile E of WOLVERGHEM.	2nd Jt Sqn
4–11–14.	1 Troop completed work on same line.	
5–11–14.	Remained in billets.	
6–11–14.		
7–11–14.	Two Troops out all night to work on same line. No work necessary except 1 barricade	
8–11–14.		
9–11–14	Remained at St Jans Cappel. Entrenchments with Flares etc	
10–11–14	At S. Jans Cappel, worked all night helping Transport of VII th Divn	
11–11–14	up. Front Row.	

Army Form C. 2118.

WAR DIARY
or
INTELLIGENCE SUMMARY.
(Erase heading not required.)

Instructions regarding War Diaries and Intelligence Summaries are contained in F.S. Regs., Part II. and the Staff Manual respectively. Title pages will be prepared in manuscript.

Hour, Date, Place	Summary of Events and Information	Remarks and references to Appendices
Sec 8. 12.11.14	Remained at St Jans Cappel.	2 " " 28. 50
13.11.14.	Went out & helped entrench Artillery	
14.11.14.	Reached St Thomas, near Vieux Berquin	
15.11.14	at Vieux Berquin	
16.11.14	" " "	
17.11.14	" " "	
18.11.14	" " "	
19.11.14	To strengthen line north of Kemmel by 6 hards Road	
20.11.14	with 2 rive & 4 p.m. to 10 a.m.	
21.11.14	as for 20th	
22.11.14	Fire taken over by 1st Div.	
23.11.14	Entering loopholes from Steenflakes to Bailleul	
24.11.14	at Vieux Berquin.	

Army Form C. 2118.

WAR DIARY
or
INTELLIGENCE SUMMARY.

(Erase heading not required.)

Instructions regarding War Diaries and Intelligence Summaries are contained in F.S. Regs., Part II. and the Staff Manual respectively. Title pages will be prepared in manuscript.

Hour, Date, Place	Summary of Events and Information	Remarks and references to Appendices
25. 11. 14	Remained at Vieux Berquin. All men employed on erecting mud screens & temporary shelters for horses of the Division.	
26. 11. 14		
27. 11. 14		
28. 11. 14		
29. 11. 14		
30. 11. 14		

Stevens Capt RE
O.C. 2'd Sig. Coy RE
2. XII. 14

2nd Cavalry Divisional Engineers

2nd FIELD SQUADRON R. E.

DECEMBER 1914.

WAR DIARY
or
INTELLIGENCE SUMMARY.

(Erase heading not required.)

Army Form C. 2118.

2nd Fd Sy Mn RE — Summary of Events and Information — 2nd Cav Div

Hour, Date, Place		Remarks and references to Appendices

Dec 1 – 31 | At "VIEUX BERQUIN" [NORD]

Coohpies in

(1) making model trenches and instructing comdr in use & instruction of same

(2) making bomb guns & hand grenades & ex plaining use of same to cavalry

(3) erection & maintenance of wire screens for horses etc.

Dec 23 { went L/H Simn RE Journal
 { Capt L. Chevaux Trench RE tramjeny
  to 3rd Fd Sqdn.

2nd Cavalry Division

121/4259

2nd Field Squadron R.E.

Vol VI. 1 — 31.1.15

Nil

WAR DIARY
or
INTELLIGENCE SUMMARY.

(Erase heading not required.)

Army Form C. 2118.

2nd Fd Sqn RE   2nd Cav Divs

Hour, Date, Place	Summary of Events and Information	Remarks and references to Appendices

Jan 1 at Vieux Berguin.
    2
    3

1. Sqn remains at Vieux Berquin.
2. 3 troop & all Officers proceed to billet at HINGES
3. Capt C.R. Johnson 280 R.E. admitting to hospital with dislocated rib. Lieut V H Sim assumes command of unit
4. The O.C. 2 Fd Sqn takes charge of 2nd line defences & "points d'appui", & 3rd line defences, of 1st Corps, working under the C.E. 1st Corps. All ranks employed in supervision of French civil labour — about 1500 employed.

Army Form C. 2118.

WAR DIARY
or
INTELLIGENCE SUMMARY.
(Erase heading not required.)

Instructions regarding War Diaries and Intelligence Summaries are contained in F.S. Regs., Part II. and the Staff Manual respectively. Title pages will be prepared in manuscript.

Hour, Date, Place	Summary of Events and Information	Remarks and references to Appendices
Jan 5th – 31st.	Officers, N.C.Os and men of the unit employed superintending the labour of 2NRs 1500 increasing eventually to 2600 civilian on the 2nd line defences E and N.E of BETHUNE for the 1st Army Corps; also on the 3rd line of defence along the LA BASSEE canal. The work carried out consisted of 10 closed work, 1 blockhouse, 5 miles of breastwork with bridge heads in advance, the making of 2 preserve roads each ½ mile long and the clearage and trolleying of an aerodrome.	
Jan 23rd	MAJOR C.R. JOHNSON R.E. returned to command the unit, on discharge from hospital.	
Jan 31st.	The unit returned to VIEUX BERQUIN.	

C.R. Johnson
Major R.E.
O.C. 2nd Field Company R.E.

121/4634

2nd Cavalry Division

2nd Field Squadron R.E.

Vol VII. 1 – 28.2.15.

121/4634

Army Form C. 2118.

WAR DIARY
or
INTELLIGENCE SUMMARY.
(Erase heading not required.)

Instructions regarding War Diaries and Intelligence Summaries are contained in F.S. Regs., Part II. and the Staff Manual respectively. Title pages will be prepared in manuscript.

Hour, Date, Place	Summary of Events and Information	Remarks and references to Appendices
Feb 1st — 11th	The novel was employed making the cavalry regiment in the valley and east of hand grenades. The manufacture of bomb guns and ammunition was continued. Capt. F. PREEDY joined the 11th Level S.o R.E.	
Feb 8th	2nd Lt. A.V.D. Wise joined the 2nd Field Squadron R.E.	
Feb 10th		
Feb 12th — 23rd	In the trenches S.E. of YPRES. The work carried out consisted of chiefly:- (a) Strengthening parapet where old & old lay (b) Repairing parapet (c) Drainage (d) Wire entanglement. (e) Digging two redoubts to hold 20 men each as supporting points to our line of defence. (f) Provision of hand grenades and bomb ammunition for guns made by 2nd Field Squadron.	

Forms/C. 2118/10

Army Form C. 2118.

WAR DIARY
or
INTELLIGENCE SUMMARY.
(Erase heading not required.)

Instructions regarding War Diaries and Intelligence Summaries are contained in F.S. Regs., Part II. and the Staff Manual respectively. Title pages will be prepared in manuscript.

Hour, Date, Place	Summary of Events and Information	Remarks and references to Appendices
Feb 21st	The Germans exploded a mine in the end of the front trench near our communication trench. As the point had been suspected a new cavalier trench had been made in rear but apparently was never occupied being in the communication trench that follows. The 16th Lancers lost heavily in the attack. During the 10 days the unit was in the trenches the casualties were 2 killed and 3 wounded.	
Feb 24th – 26th	At VIEUX BERQUIN resting	
Feb 27th – 28th	At HERVARRE resting.	

2nd Field Squadron R.E.

Part VIII 1 – 31.3.15

2nd Cavalry Division

Army Form C. 2118.

WAR DIARY
or
INTELLIGENCE SUMMARY.
(Erase heading not required.)

2nd Field Squadron R.E.

Instructions regarding War Diaries and Intelligence Summaries are contained in F.S. Regs., Part II. and the Staff Manual respectively. Title pages will be prepared in manuscript.

Hour, Date, Place	Summary of Events and Information	Remarks and references to Appendices
March 1st	At HERVARRE resting.	
March 2nd to March 8th	At CAUCHY D'ECQUES	
March 4th	Capt. V.H. SIMON R.E. joined and took over 3rd Field Squadron R.E.	
March 9th to March 22nd	Billets at LA COURONNE - VIEUX BERQUIN	
March 10th to March 13th	Standing by in connection with attack at NEUVE CHAPELLE	
March 12th	Lt. W.P. MULLIGAN R.A.M.C. transferred to No 5 Cavalry Field Ambulance; Lt. W. LUMLEY R.A.M.C. transferred from that unit to the unit.	
March 14th and March 15th	Instruction in trench storming given to SHERWOOD FORESTER Bde. (T.F.)	
March 18th	New 3½" trench gun storming a bomb of 20 lb. weight tried and found very efficient. This gun was made by the Unit.	

Forms/C. 2118/10

Army Form C. 2118.

WAR DIARY
or
INTELLIGENCE SUMMARY.
(Erase heading not required.) 2nd Bn. Ct Yorksh. R.E. (2)

Instructions regarding War Diaries and Intelligence Summaries are contained in F.S. Regs., Part II. and the Staff Manual respectively. Title pages will be prepared in manuscript.

Hour, Date, Place	Summary of Events and Information	Remarks and references to Appendices
March 18th to March 20th	Instruction in bomb throwing given to 4th Early Brigade.	
March 19th and March 20th	Further instruction in bomb throwing given to SHERWOOD FORESTERS Bde (T.F.)	
March 21st	Engineer reconnaissance to NEUVE CHAPELLE and neighbourhood by 3 officers.	
March 23rd to March 31st	Billets N of VIEUX BERQUIN	
March 22nd to March 31st	Instruction in bomb throwing given to 3rd Early Brigade.	
March 22nd	Instruction in the use of earthrop given to SHERWOOD FORESTERS Bde (T.F.)	
March 25th	Engineer reconnaissance by O.C. L FAUQUISSART Engineer reconnaissance by 3 officers to NEUVE CHAPELLE and neighbourhood.	

Army Form C. 2118.

WAR DIARY
or
INTELLIGENCE SUMMARY.
(Erase heading not required.)

2nd Field Squadron R.E.

Instructions regarding War Diaries and Intelligence Summaries are contained in F.S. Regs., Part II. and the Staff Manual respectively. Title pages will be prepared in manuscript.

Hour, Date, Place	Summary of Events and Information	Remarks and references to Appendices
March 1st to March 2nd	At HERVARRE resting	
March 2nd to March 8th	At CAUCHY D'ECQUES	
March 8th	Capt. V.H. SIMON R.E. joins and to join 3rd Field Squadron R.E.	
March 9th to March 22nd	Billets at LA COURONNE VIEUX-BERQUIN	
March 10th to March 13th	Standing by in case to collect wire at NEUVE CHAPELLE	
March 12th	Lt. W.P. MULLIGAN R.A.M.C. transferred to No 5 Cavalry Field Ambulance; Lt. W.W. LUMLEY R.A.M.C. transferred from that unit to this unit	
March 14th and March 15th	Instruction in trench storm guns to SHERWOOD FORESTER Bde (T.F.)	
March 18th	New 5½" Trench gun firing a load of 20 lb. weight tried and found very efficient. This gun was made by the Sqdn.	

Army Form C. 2118.

WAR DIARY
or
INTELLIGENCE SUMMARY.
(Erase heading not required.) 2nd Field Squadron R.E.

(2)

Hour, Date, Place	Summary of Events and Information	Remarks and references to Appendices
March 18th	Instruction in boat throwing given to 4th	
to March 20th	Cavalry Brigade.	
March 19th and March 20th	Further instruction in boat throwing given to SHERWOOD FORESTERS Bde (T.F.)	
March 21st	Engineer reconnaissance to NEUVE CHAPELLE and neighbourhood by 3 officers.	
March 23rd to March 31st	Billets N of VIEUX BERQUIN	
March 22nd to March 23rd	Instruction in boat throwing given to 3rd Cavalry Brigade.	
March 24th	Instruction in the use of sandbags given to SHERWOOD FORESTERS Bde (T.F.)	
March 25th	Engineer reconnaissance by O.C. to FAUQUISSART Engineer reconnaissance by 3 officers to NEUVE CHAPELLE and neighbourhood.	

Army Form C. 2118.

(3) 2nd Field Squadron R.E.

WAR DIARY
or
INTELLIGENCE SUMMARY.
(Erase heading not required.)

Hour, Date, Place	Summary of Events and Information	Remarks and references to Appendices
March 26th to March 31st	Preparing stores and material and stores for boats; also collecting sandbags etc. for coming operations. Engineer reconnaissance to FACQUISSART by O.C. No 17048 Sapper A GUY R.E. awarded D.C.M. for bravery at YPRES on 22.2.15.	
March 30th		

31.3.15 VERLINGHEM
VIEUX BERQUIN

H.R. Johnson Lt
OC 2nd Field Squadron R.E.

121/5320

2nd Cavalry Division

2nd Field Squadron R.E.

Vol IX 3 — 30.4.15

Army Form C. 2118.

WAR DIARY
or
INTELLIGENCE SUMMARY
(Erase heading not required.)

Instructions regarding War Diaries and Intelligence Summaries are contained in F. S. Regs., Part II. and the Staff Manual respectively. Title pages will be prepared in manuscript.

Hour, Date, Place	Summary of Events and Information	Remarks and references to Appendices
April 3.	Instructed No15 Wellesh Div Cyclist Coy in trench digging.	
" 6" 8"	Lectures to officers & N.C.O's of VearReserves.	
	Attended K.N.B.G.ebus.	
	took a hedge to remove	
" 9" – 22"	Work on bridges, boat gear etc as usual	
" 17"	2nd Lt G.E. GRIMSDALE left Squadron to become A.D.C.	
" 23"	Marched to BOESCHEPPE and fighting portion of squadron.	
" 24"	Marched to VLAMERTINGHE where squadron bivouced.	
" 25"	Entrenched 4th Cavalry Brigade in front of BOESINGHE. Bivouced at VLAMERTINGHE.	

Army Form C. 2118.

WAR DIARY
or
INTELLIGENCE SUMMARY
(Erase heading not required.)

Instructions regarding War Diaries and Intelligence Summaries are contained in F. S. Regs., Part II. and the Staff Manual respectively. Title pages will be prepared in manuscript.

Hour, Date, Place	Summary of Events and Information	Remarks and references to Appendices
April 26th	Improved G.H.Q. defence line 1 mile east of MENIN GATE, YPRES. Casualties 1 N.C.O. killed 2 men wounded. Bivouacked at VLAMMERTINGE	
April 27th	During the day work as for April 26th	
April 28th	During the night improved arming pits & camps on switch line from HOOGE — VERLORENHOEK or switch line from HOOGE — VERLORENHOEK — WIELTJE. Bivouacked at HOOGE.	
April 29th	Continued work on HOOGE — VERLORENHOEK — WIELTJE. Continued work as for April 28th. Bivouacked at HOOGE.	
April 30th	Employed on new switch line south of HOOGE. Work chiefly on newly gained ground. Bivouacked at HOOGE.	
	B. Echelon of the unit remained at VIEUX BERQUIN during the whole month.	W.R. Johnson RE. Major O.C. 2nd Field Sqdn RE.

137/5610

2nd Cavalry Division

2nd Field Squadron R.E.

Vol X 1 — 31.5.15

Army Form C. 2118.

WAR DIARY
or
INTELLIGENCE SUMMARY

(Erase heading not required.)

Instructions regarding War Diaries and Intelligence Summaries are contained in F. S. Regs., Part II. and the Staff Manual respectively. Title pages will be prepared in manuscript.

Hour, Date, Place	Summary of Events and Information	Remarks and references to Appendices
MAY. 1st	Continued work on outlet line south of HOOGE. during the day. At night employed working parties of infantry. Bivouaced at HOOGE	
" 2nd 3rd	Work as for the 1st. Bivouaced at HOOGE. 1 man wounded during day. At night demolished Work so far provided during 2nd & 3rd. 1 N.C.O. + 1 man provided dummy dug. 150 yards of enemy parapet with 30 charges of guncotton each charge being 16 lb. 20 were fired by electricity and 10 by safety fuze. Demolition successful. Bivouaced at VLAMMERTINGHE.	
" 4th	Rested at VLAMMERTINGHE.	
" 5th	Employed on new outlet line from MENIN GATE YPRES — LILLE GATE — CANAL south of YPRES Early working party. Bivouaced at VLAMMERTINGHE	
" 6th	As for the 5th. " "	
" 7th	" " " Started work on supporting points to line	

Army Form C. 2118.

WAR DIARY
or
INTELLIGENCE SUMMARY
(Erase heading not required.)

Instructions regarding War Diaries and Intelligence Summaries are contained in F. S. Regs., Part II. and the Staff Manual respectively. Title pages will be prepared in manuscript.

Hour, Date, Place	Summary of Events and Information	Remarks and references to Appendices
May 8th " 9th	Returned to VIEUX BERQUIN. Sent 2 off. & 16' bridges down roads leading to Neuf Berquin to houses at 1 cross on Rue TILLELOY 3/4 mile NE of FAUQUISSART.	
10th – 12th	Rep. Hd.	
13th	Ordered (9pm) to concentrate above	
14th	Embussed 2am. Arrived VLAMERTINGHE 6am. 2nd Lt. Sr. Wood 1st Coy in trenches E of POTIJZE.	
	2.30 pm. Squadron employed superintending working party of 800 men and erecting wire entanglement. 1 man wounded.	
15th	Erecting wire entanglement by night. 1 man killed.	
16th	Erecting wire entanglement by night and 2 supporting points by day.	
17th	Same as for 16th.	
18th	Erecting wire entanglement in front of 1st line and employed on 2nd line of defence (G.H.Q line)	

WAR DIARY
or
INTELLIGENCE SUMMARY.
(Erase heading not required.)

Army Form C. 2118.

Hour, Date, Place	Summary of Events and Information	Remarks and references to Appendices
May 19th	Employed on 2nd line defences improving & wiring the same. Same as for 19th.	
20th & 21st		
22nd to 25th inclusive	Employed on 3rd line defences i.e. canal line N & S of YPRES and ramparts of YPRES. Working pty of 300 Belgians. Work carried out consisted of (a) Infantry making firing & supporting trench tracks, making cover trenches and communication tracks. (b) Infantry wire entanglement. (c) Clearing foreground in front of 1st line tracks. (d) Making M.G. emplacements on ramparts with communication tracks. (e) Clearing foreground in front of retrenchment i.e. trimming and demolishing houses. (f) Loopholing houses.	
May 25th	2nd Cavy Division returned to the tracks. At night had 500 infantry for digging 2nd line of defence. Igordoes employed wiring the line.	

Army Form C. 2118.

WAR DIARY
or
INTELLIGENCE SUMMARY.
(Erase heading not required.)

Instructions regarding War Diaries and Intelligence Summaries are contained in F.S. Regs., Part II. and the Staff Manual respectively. Title pages will be prepared in manuscript.

Hour, Date, Place	Summary of Events and Information	Remarks and references to Appendices
May 26th	At night had working party of 600 employed on 2nd line trenches and communication trenches. Erected wire entanglement round houses of HOOGE village consisting N of road.	
27th	Preparing houses in HOOGE village for a shell-proof defence. Also on a supporting point in rear of 2nd line trenches.	
28th	Resting	
29th	2nd Cavalry Division relieved at 9 p.m. Field Squadron entrained for VIEUX BERQUIN at 7.15 p.m. Arrived 10 p.m. at old billets.	
30th	Resting	
31st	Marched at 8.15 a.m. for new billets near EBBLINGHEM arrived at 11.30 a.m. (12 miles)	

E.R. Johnson
Major 3rd Field Sqdn 2nd July 15
O.C. 2. F.S.

2nd Cavalry Division.

12/6358

June-July 1915

2nd Field Squadron R.E.

Vol XL

WAR DIARY
or
INTELLIGENCE SUMMARY.

Army Form C. 2118.

(Erase heading not required.)

Hour, Date, Place	Summary of Events and Information	Remarks and references to Appendices
June 1–17.	Billets at EBBLINGHEM. Work consisted of — a) Some practice bridges for spans on Canal b) Work at Trades 1725 c) Instruction to Cavalry in front. Storming trench mortar use.	
18.	A serious accident occurred while 20th Pack was in shooting. 20th Hussars in throwing down a bomb from trench to trench. Party (parade) of 20th Pack – 2 bay. – One man + 2 trench mortars. For some reason which cannot be discovered a trench (C.I. cylindrical battle) exploded on the hands of the thrower. Killing him (thrower) 1st Park the 3 other men of 2nd Park + men of 20th Hussars. 4 RA died in hospital. Continued instruction to Cavalry in trench mortary &c	
19th – 22nd	Classes held for pioneers of Cavalry Regts. including preliminary instruction in revolvers. Labor laying dummy charges in site on a front. Ridge + on a Railway line.	
23rd – 29th	70 N.C.O.s men marched to DICKEBUSH to reinforced a digging party of 1600 Cavalry.	

30.

WAR DIARY
or
INTELLIGENCE SUMMARY.
(Erase heading not required.)

Army Form C. 2118.

Hour, Date, Place	Summary of Events and Information	Remarks and references to Appendices
July 1st – 31st	1800 men of the 2nd Kings Division have been placed under the orders of 2nd Army for digging. The work consists of (a) placing localities in a state of defence (b) adding strongpoints to existing lines (c) repairing & lengthening existing lines of trenches. Work was started in 8 places as follows: (i) Chateau 1.19.c (ii) Chateau H.24.c ; H.30.a & d. (iii) Farm H.27.c (iv) Farm H.26.d. (v) Farm H.26.c (vi) G.H.Q. line H.31.a.c (vii) Locality H.32.c. (St HUBERTSHOEK) (viii) Locality H.32.d and N.3.c. (HALLEBAST) These works were completed about July 18th. Further work was started at the following places. (i) LA CLYTTE N.7.a (ii) Farm N.7.d. (iii) Farm N.14.a These works were completed about July 30th. Work is now proceeding at the following places	Sheet 28

WAR DIARY
or
INTELLIGENCE SUMMARY.
(Erase heading not required.)

Army Form C. 2118.

Hour, Date, Place	Summary of Events and Information	Remarks and references to Appendices
July 1st – 31st	(i) From M.12.c. (ii) Locality M.18.a (SCHERPENBERG)	
July 1st – 18th	(iii) From N.13.a,c (iv) From N.20.a (v) Locality N.20.B.	
July 19th – 31st	(vi) G.H.Q.2 line N.20.B.d. (vii) KEMMEL N.21.c	
	(viii) Reberchuck N.31.a.B.; 32.a.; 26.B.c.d.	
	Billets of B Section at EBBLINGHEM	
	4 Officers + 70 N.C.Os + men bivouced at farm H.22.c.	
	" " N.13.a.c.	
July 24th	Lt. S.J. Armstrong R.E. joined the unit	

J.R. Johnson
Major R.E.
O.C. 2nd Field Squadron R.E.

12/6769.

2nd Cavalry Division

No 2 Field Squadron R.E.

Lt Sill.

August 1. 15

Army Form C. 2118.

WAR DIARY
or
INTELLIGENCE SUMMARY
(Erase heading not required.)

Hour, Date, Place	Summary of Events and Information	Remarks and references to Appendices
AUGUST	Major C.R. Johnson D.S.O. R.E. (OC), Capt. T.A.S. Swinburne, Lt. A.M. Carnduff, Lt. S.J. Armstrong, Lt. A.V.D. Wise, Lt. & Lt. R.D. Waghorn, and 70 N.C.O.s & men of the unit were employed during the month superintending the work of 1000 men of the 2nd Cavalry Division who were employed on the defence of localities in the 2nd & 3rd Corps rear areas. The area of the 2nd & 3rd Corps was changed during the early part of August and work was completed to the satisfaction of the 2nd & 3rd Corps areas. The G.O.C. 3rd Corps having different ideas of field & personal fortification to those entertained by the G.O.C. 2nd Corps, before taking over certain works. Operations extensive alterations in the Ypres canal bank (A) Completed clearing out canals (B) Revetting bay there (C) Dug out shelters of strong splinter proof (D) Carry on all communication trenches (E) to make all works close anywhere with new work on 2nd Corps area awaiting On completion of work on 2nd Corps area work of making fully bore return to this original work in the 3rd Corps area	[Stamp: O.C. 2nd Field Squadron Royal Engineers]

Army Form C. 2118.

WAR DIARY
or
INTELLIGENCE SUMMARY

(Erase heading not required.)

Instructions regarding War Diaries and Intelligence Summaries are contained in F. S. Regs., Part II. and the Staff Manual respectively. Title pages will be prepared in manuscript.

Hour, Date, Place	Summary of Events and Information	Remarks and references to Appendices
AUGUST 6th	H.Q. of the unit was moved from EBBLINGHEM to ROQUETOIRE WEST. The working party was billeted for the whole month out from N 13 A.C. The G.O.C. of Rouen has conferred the Order of St STANISLAS 3rd Class with swords on Major C.R. JOHNSON D.S.O. R.E. and the Medal of St GEORGE 2nd Class on No. 28910 S.Q.M.S. H. POWELL R.E. also the Medal of St GEORGE 4th Class on Nos. 16702 2nd Cpl. P. McGINNIS R.E. 17143 2nd Cpl. S. MORGAN R.E.	[stamp: 2nd Field Company Royal Engineers] R.R. Johnson Lt. Col. R.E. O.C. 2nd Field Company R.E. 8.9.15

12/7/53

2nd Cavalry Division

2nd Field Squadn R.E.

for XIII

Sept 15

Army Form C. 2118.

WAR DIARY
or
INTELLIGENCE SUMMARY

(Erase heading not required.)

Instructions regarding War Diaries and Intelligence Summaries are contained in F. S. Regs., Part II. and the Staff Manual respectively. Title pages will be prepared in manuscript.

Hour, Date, Place	Summary of Events and Information	Remarks and references to Appendices
SEPTEMBER		
1st — 4th	The digging parties of the 2nd Cavalry Division continued their work near KEMMEL and DICKEBUSH; they returning to their billets on the 4th. All works were handed over to Infantry Division occupying the area concerned.	
5th	Officers and men of the Field Squadron reorganised. H.Q. at ROQUETOIRE.	
6th — 14th	Riding drill for recruits. Practice with and alterations to new boat equipment.	
15th	Field day with collapsible boat equipment. Bridge formed across canal at WARDRECQUES 70 feet wide. 5th Cavalry Bde passed over bridge in 1½ hours; this included M.G. limbers which were wonderfully clever. Average time per squadron = 7 minutes.	

Army Form C. 2118.

WAR DIARY
or
INTELLIGENCE SUMMARY

(Erase heading not required.)

Hour, Date, Place	Summary of Events and Information	Remarks and references to Appendices
	In the afternoon spans of the 3rd and 4th Bdes passed over bridge. In all about 2500 horses crossed the bridge without the slightest accident. At night 5th Cavalry Bde had a relow involving the passage of the canal. No. 1 & 2 troops R.E. were employed. 7 obstacles had to be crossed of which the R.E. trestles 5 i.e. ditch, canal, steep clip, telegraph line and ditch. The canal bridge was completed in 12 hours and the remaining obstacles overcome 1 hour later. The Brigade took 24 hours to cross by night but could do it in quicker time. No horse or man made a mistake crossing the bridge. The night was dark.	

Instructions regarding War Diaries and Intelligence Summaries are contained in F. S. Regs., Part II. and the Staff Manual respectively. Title pages will be prepared in manuscript.

Army Form C. 2118.

WAR DIARY
or
INTELLIGENCE SUMMARY

(Erase heading not required.)

Instructions regarding War Diaries and Intelligence Summaries are contained in F. S. Regs, Part II. and the Staff Manual respectively. Title pages will be prepared in manuscript.

Hour, Date, Place	Summary of Events and Information	Remarks and references to Appendices
16th – 19th	Demolitions with Brigade.	
20th – 22nd	Erection at DELETTES of portable steel girder bridge. C in C and D.D.W. were present. The Squadron gained a working knowledge necessary for the erection of this type of bridge.	
23rd – 24th	Billetted at FLEURY	
25th	Unit marched to MARLES LES MINES where it remained until 28th.	
29th	Unit marched to FERFAY (FOSSE 1 mile N.E.)	
30th	At the FOSSE mentioned above	

14.10.15.

E.R. Johnson
Major R.E.
O.C. 2nd Field Squadron R.E.

121/7599

G.S. 2nd ft. C. Rt.

Oct 1915

Vol III XI

Army Form C. 2118.

WAR DIARY
or
INTELLIGENCE SUMMARY
(Erase heading not required.)

Instructions regarding War Diaries and Intelligence Summaries are contained in F. S. Regs., Part II. and the Staff Manual respectively. Title pages will be prepared in manuscript.

Hour, Date, Place	Summary of Events and Information	Remarks and references to Appendices
October 1	Billets FERFAY.	
2 – 6	70 men went up into Captured German trenches between VERMELLES LAVENTIE. They were employed under C.E. II Corps to try to make the infantry took up parties in reconnoitring old German trenches. Shocking his flank trenches, Sergt FOSS & Corporal Lieut T.J. LATHAM R.E. mé killed. 4 men wounded. Returned to force near FERFAY.	
7 – 16	Billets FERFAY. Captain SWINBURNE R.E. appointed Divisional Bomb Officer.	
17	Unit returned to old billets in ROQUETOIRE	
19	Unit marched to new billets at WILLAMETZ	
25	Unit marched to billets near LA NIEPPE as Aisne (Operations start soon).	

WAR DIARY
or
INTELLIGENCE SUMMARY
(Erase heading not required.)

Army Form C. 2118

Place	Date	Hour	Summary of Events and Information	Remarks and references to Appendices
	October 25		2nd Lt. HAGHORN & 20 men left for work in trenches wh. Labour Battalion on B.C.D line near FRUGES.	
	30		3rd B&e cutting paths began work in the wood at DROUVILLE	

J. Humphries
Capt R.E.
O.C. 2nd Fd Sqn

8th Schumann

2. p. Sap. R.
2/1915
XII

7655
/c/

WAR DIARY
or
INTELLIGENCE SUMMARY
(Erase heading not required.)

Army Form. C. 2118

Place	Date	Hour	Summary of Events and Information	Remarks and references to Appendices
	November 1.		Work commenced with 800 men on G.H.Q. 4th line of defence from LE METRE - EBBLINGHEM (road) to high grounds ½ mile to S.E. Strong defended localities started at LE METRE, T.18.b. & EBBLINGHEM (road). Other strong hunters had given an by Can. Corps. 1. Dig out 5 ft. 11". wire. iii line. Strong points for the Comm- -plete front then one but along the whole line. Capt. T.A Montoure appointed Chevalier of the Legion of Honour. "4th Class"	
	7.		Working Parties have gradually increased to maximum of 2000 men per regiment. Some extensive work made taken	
	8 to 30.		.. at the end of the month the strength of the Divisional Working Party was about 1450 men.	

Army Form C. 2118

WAR DIARY
or
INTELLIGENCE SUMMARY

(Erase heading not required.)

Instructions regarding War Diaries and Intelligence Summaries are contained in F. S. Regs., Part II. and the Staff Manual respectively. Title Pages will be prepared in manuscript.

Place	Date	Hour	Summary of Events and Information	Remarks and references to Appendices
	November 29.		Lt Wayhorn's party with the exception of Lt Wayhorn returned the unit from AUDINGTHUN. During the whole of this month, Major C.R. Johnson D.S.O R.E. has been of O.R.S. to Cavalry Corps. T. Sherbrooke Capt	

2nd FIELD SQUADRON
ROYAL ENGINEERS

2nd Cav

No. 2 Fd. Sqn. R.E.
Dec 1915.
Vol XVI

WAR DIARY or INTELLIGENCE SUMMARY

Army Form C. 2118

Place	Date	Hour	Summary of Events and Information	Remarks and references to Appendices
LE MISPPE	December 1 – 27		Sapping operations proceeded throughout the month (as stated), but the frequent very very wet weather proper was also. The weather throughout the month was very bad.	
	28.		Sapping parties were suddenly withdrawn at 12 hours notice. All material has to be left behind. 20 men Unicorn to collect stones & carry or cart on say out if possible. Remainder of present marches to WILLAMETZ.	
	29.		From 12 noon entrenchment division to at 3½ hours notice to move.	
	30.			
	31.		Party for Dismounted Divn :- strength 3 officers, 50 men, proceeded to WIZERNES, entrained to fillers. Pollets Bgs. RIEUX. During the month of December Major C R Johnson acted as C.R.E. Cav Corps. R.K.Wrighton for O.C. 2nd Fd Sqdn RE	

Army Form C. 2118

WAR DIARY
or
INTELLIGENCE SUMMARY
(Erase heading not required.)

Place	Date	Hour	Summary of Events and Information	Remarks and references to Appendices
WILLAMETZ	January 1916 1 – 31st		Throughout this month the Bienvillers Troop remained in three billets. Lieut R.D. WAGHORN R.E. was employed on temporary work with the 9th Station Battalion, near AUDINGHUN He replaced the being relieved in January by Lieut J.J. ARMSTRONG R.E. who came back from the Bienvillers Troop. L. STAGHORN rejoined Bienvillers Troop. 1 Sapper & 9 O.R. were employed on the LE NIEPPE line putting trenches into such a state that they could be left without fear further deterioration. 18.1.16 Lt. J.F. FORSYTH R.E. T.C. joined Bienvillers Troop 20.1.16 2nd Lt. F.G. THOMAS	

J Longman
H.H. Capt

O.C. 2nd FIELD SQUADRON
ROYAL ENGINEERS

WAR DIARY
or
INTELLIGENCE SUMMARY

Army Form C. 2118

(Erase heading not required.)

Place	Date	Hour	Summary of Events and Information	Remarks and references to Appendices
# MILLAM (?)	Feb. 1 - 15.	15.	Squadron less Observers detachment & party at Le NIEPPE remained in billets.	
	16 - 29.		Afterwards Troop returned from LA PHILOSOPHE. Training of Unit in Field works proceeded. Subjects fire trench, Demolitions, Spars, Bridges, ongoing work was through, interfered with by bad weather rarely. Throughout the month Major C.R. JOHNSON D.S.O. R.E. acted as C.R.E. Can Corps from 1.2.16 to 15.2.16 to discounts by. from 16.2.16 to 29.2.16 5 Can Corps.	

A. Woodward
Capt.

WAR DIARY or INTELLIGENCE SUMMARY

Army Form C. 2118

Place	Date	Hour	Summary of Events and Information	Remarks and references to Appendices
WILLA METZ	March 1916			
	1 - 5		Spring training was commenced. Every two weeks taken here. Kestrey & Lashey. Use of spars, flasks & tackles. Trestle bridge. Revolution of gunnery frames.	
	6 - 12		Subjects taken were Boat Drill, Lock Bridges, Voyageur trench. Preliminary Musketry has commenced including care of arms, aiming &c.	
	13 - 19		All troops carried out a small bridging scheme over river near FOURENBERGUES, two troops. Another day about ferry from 5 boats. Drill on the river. Musketry instruction in Fire Positions, Fire Discipline marched two files & standard trots were begun.	
	20 - 31		Musketry was carried out on a range up to 200°. All troops were also practised in simple drill for getting up rapid wire entanglement at night.	

J. Whitehouse
Captain R.E.
O.C. 2nd F.S.

WAR DIARY or INTELLIGENCE SUMMARY

Army Form C. 2118

Place	Date	Hour	Summary of Events and Information	Remarks and references to Appendices
WILLAMETZ	April 1916			
	1st – 10th		Troops & H.Q. Officers went through Riding Instruction. Also Infantry Drill. Collapsible bridges for crossing trenches were improvised & tested.	
	12th		Major C.R. Johnson L.O. R.E. was struck by the shaft of a limber passing by & had fractured base of skull.	
	13th – 30th		Riding School continued. N.C.O.'s & men have constantly been invited to map reading & sketching. Frequently reconnaissances in engineer took on reports.	
	5th		G.O.C 2nd Car div. inspected the horses of the Squadron.	

[Signature]
Captn. 2nd F.S.
O.C. 2nd F.S.

[Stamp: O.C. 2nd FIELD SQUADRON ROYAL ENGINEERS]

Army Form C. 2118

WAR DIARY
or
INTELLIGENCE SUMMARY
(Erase heading not required.)

Vol 20

Place	Date	Hour	Summary of Events and Information	Remarks and references to Appendices
WILLAMETZ	1-5-16		Short Pioneer course was held for 5th Cavalry Bde. 18 Officers & 12 men from each regiment. Duration of course 8 working days. Course included Sandbag work, knots, demolitions, schemes & reports & demolition of stations &c. Bridging, Expedients, knotting, lashing &c.	
	11.5.16			
	12.5.16		Moved billets to LEDINGHEM.	
LEDINGHEM	14.5.16		Course similar to that for 5th Bde was carried out with 3rd Cavalry Bde.	
	23.5.16			
	28.5.16		Similar Pioneer Course was commenced with 4th Cav Bde.	
	29.5.16		Lt Kegan R.E. & 15 O.R. proceeded to HQ Canadian Corps at ABEELE to report for work	
	30.5.16		2 Lt Thomas R.E. & 15 O.R. similarly reported to HQ I Corps at BAILLEUL. Capt Swinburne R.E. proceeded to HQ 3rd Canadian Div RENING-HELST in connection with above work.	
	31.5.16		Lt Armstrong R.E. & 12 O.R. with 12 horses proceeded to join 2nd Army School at WISQUES. Lt Armstrong to instruct him in Pioneering	T.A. Armstrong Capt R.E.

2c

2 2nd Sqn R.E.

Army Form C. 2118

WAR DIARY
or
INTELLIGENCE SUMMARY

June 1916

Place	Date	Hour	Summary of Events and Information	Remarks and references to Appendices
LEDINGHEM	June 1-9	20.17	Squadron remained in billets. The 2 parties in R. Canadian F. Coys. worked on the G.H.Q. 2 line from SWAN CH^AU & BRIDGE B on the North to KENNEL - WYTSCHAETE road on the south. Lt Thomas's detachment has been working on the defences of Kemmel village.	
	10th		From June 12-17. E. Ede & 23 C.R. joined 8th Co. R. Canadian Coys as part of 2nd Durham Brigade which has moved up to POMMINGHURST.	
	18th		All detachments rejoined H.Q. at PLOEGSTEERT except that at 2nd Army School.	
	21.		Squadron moved to AU POUVRAIN.	
	25.		Lt Armstrong's party rejoined.	
	26-30		Carried out practice bridging on LA NOTTE Canal. Fitted up 40 G.S. wagons of A.H.T. Coy to carry 200 gallon water tanks.	

A. Armstrong
Capt.

CONFIDENTIAL.

WAR DIARY

of

2nd Field Squadron. R.E.

from: 1st July   to: 31st July.1916.

(Volume XXIII.).

WAR DIARY or INTELLIGENCE SUMMARY

Army Form C. 2118

Place	Date	Hour	Summary of Events and Information	Remarks and references to Appendices
AU SOUVERAIN	July 1-31.	8.	Squadron returned to billets. Some subsections too far in rear; convoy 8th. Trestle bridging was also practised on canal. Capt Plowdrue, Lieuts Brueton, Forsyth & Thomas & 60 O.R. pro- ceeded to join Cavalry working party at la CRECHE. The whole party was employed on finishing off old Concrete O.P.s on July 63 & in commencing new ones. By the end of the month to have com- pleted 12 new in hand. This includes concrete dug-outs which were from an exposed place instead F.P.s Cavalry labour was used in excavation. Concrete-mixing was carrying to a total of 350 to 400. Cpl. Fitzgerald, Cpl. Groves, Sapper Gale & Sapper Hove evacuated wounded during this period. T. Plowdrue Capt	

CONFIDENTIAL.

WAR   DIARY   OF

2nd FIELD SQUADRON, R.E.

for August, 1916.

Vol. ~~XIV~~

Army Form C. 2118

WAR DIARY
or
INTELLIGENCE SUMMARY
(Erase heading not required.)

Instructions regarding War Diaries and Intelligence Summaries are contained in F.S. Regs., Part II. and the Staff Manual respectively. Title Pages will be prepared in manuscript.

Place	Date	Hour	Summary of Events and Information	Remarks and references to Appendices
August	1 - 31.		Squadron H.Q. remained at AU SOUVERAIN throughout the month. Capt. Strutherine and 3 other officers with about 105 O.R. worked throughout the month on O.P's on Hill 63. About 350 Cavalry were available in this week. Lt Forsyth was on the renovation of 600 yards of subsidiary line trench on N. slope of Hill 63. L' Good on section 121st Inf Coy R.E. were also employed on the line with a working party of Cavalry (when spare) from 250 to 450. The O.P's were done greatly under C.E. Corps First 5th then 9th. Trench was done under CRE 36th Divn. At the close of the month 20 concrete O.P's & 14 concrete dugouts have been completed, to 4 more O.P's to say Orders were so far advanced that 6 days more work have finished them all. 2nd Lt G.L. Kezar was evacuated sick on 6.8.16. A. Strutherine Capt C.E. O.C. 2nd	

SECRET.

Vol 24

WAR   DIARY

of

2nd   FIELD   SQUADRON,   R.E.

for September, 1916.

VOLUME ~~XXV~~.

******

WAR DIARY
INTELLIGENCE SUMMARY
(Erase heading not required.)

Army Form C. 2118

Instructions regarding War Diaries and Intelligence Summaries are contained in F.S. Regs., Part II. and the Staff Manual respectively. Title Pages will be prepared in manuscript.

Place	Date	Hour	Summary of Events and Information	Remarks and references to Appendices
Sep.	1, 2, 3		Working Party under Capt. Morehouse injured HQ from Wytschaete of A.A. 63 took up EPU line untill A week of Completion was handed over to 178th. A.T. Coy.	
	3, 4, 5 6,		Work of the remainder at AH SOUVERAIN & Retained Squadron marched to LA PIERRERIE 2 miles S.W. of ST VENANT.	
	7		" " HESTRUS	
	8		" " ERQUIERES	
	9		" " OCCOCHES	
	10		" " ½ mile S. of FRICOURT & there tents to Bivouac.	
	11 - 14		The last two branches appeared about 60 miles. Sqdn was employed with a working party from 3rd Cav Div in making tracks passable for Cavalry from MONTAUBAN, to N of DELVILLE WOOD, towards the firing line.	
	15 - 16		Infantry advanced beyond FLERS & track was pushed on behind them.	
	17 - 24		Work was continued on track, with a party of 2nd Cav Div, in place of 3rd Cav Div.	
	25 - 26		Infantry advanced beyond GUEUDECOURT & trenches were filled & we gapped as far as front line. Casualties during this operation killed 2 O.R. 3 O.R.	
	26th		Divisional Officer complimented field Squadron & working party on the excellent work done on the Cavalry Track. R Echelon moved back to BONNAY on 15th & rejoined Sqn near FRICOURT on 28th.	

SECRET.

WAR DIARY

of

2nd FIELD SQUADRON, R.E.

OCTOBER, 1916.

VOL. XXVI.

WAR DIARY
or
INTELLIGENCE SUMMARY

(Erase heading not required.)

Army Form C. 2118

Instructions regarding War Diaries and Intelligence Summaries are contained in F.S. Regs., Part II. and the Staff Manual respectively. Title Pages will be prepared in manuscript.

Place	Date	Hour	Summary of Events and Information	Remarks and references to Appendices
FRICOURT.	Oct 1 - 9th		Whole Squadron was employed on construction of 3 water-points each for a Cavalry Division, 1 at TREUX, 1 at VILLE Sous CORBIE & 1 at BERNAFAY WOOD.	
	10 - 14th		Another water-point was constructed at LINK ROAD - S.E. of FRICOURT.	
	15 - 23rd		A working party of 2nd Cavalry was employed on maintenance of Cavalry Tracks. After this date heather wickers had to be used that work on them became nearly impossible.	
	23rd - 26th		A plank track was commenced to enable RHA to get forward along East edge of Happy Wood but was abandoned owing to inability to get forward of RHA.	
	27th - 31st		Nothing to report.	

5-11-16. A Bouchant Capt

O.C. 2nd F.S.

SECRET.

WAR DIARY

of

2nd FIELD SQUADRON, R.E.

NOVEMBER, 1916.

VOL. XXVII.

WAR DIARY
INTELLIGENCE SUMMARY
(Erase heading not required.)

Army Form C. 2118.

Instructions regarding War Diaries and Intelligence Summaries are contained in F.S. Regs., Part II. and the Staff Manual respectively. Title Pages will be prepared in manuscript.

Place	Date	Hour	Summary of Events and Information	Remarks and references to Appendices
FRICOURT.	Nov. 1st – 7th		Squadron remained in huts at Fricourt. Personnel wounded.	
	8th		Left Somme area. Marched to BUSSY near DAOURS. Bivouacked.	
	9th		Marched via Amiens to FLIXECOURT. Billeted.	
	10th		" to PONT LE GRAND - BUTLERS ABBEVILLE. Bivouacked under huts.	
	11th		" CRECY to DOURIEZ. Bivouacked under huts.	
	12th – 18th		Settled into huts & started work on Divisional School. Preparing classrooms. Making furniture &c.	
	19th		Left No 1 & 2 Troops in DOURIEZ. No 3 to BONCHES & HQ to ESTRUVAL, to clear BOURES for the School.	
	23rd		Lt G.L. KEZAR. Ngoming from England.	
	26.		Informed that Division will shortly move South. Training to be suspended.	
	12th – 26th		Small parties been attached to Cavalry units to assist them in the erection of huts & stabling.	

M. Montague
Capt R.E.
O.C. 2nd F.S.Sqn

CONFIDENTIAL.

WAR DIARY

of

2nd FIELD SQUADRON, R.E.

DECEMBER, 1916.

VOL. XXVIII.

WAR DIARY or INTELLIGENCE SUMMARY

Army Form C. 2118

Place	Date	Hour	Summary of Events and Information	Remarks and references to Appendices
	December 1916		Throughout the month the Squadron was in billets at DOURIEZ - ESTRUVAL & PONCHES. No detachments were sent away. Considerable work was done in the way of military duties & improving billet accommodation for units.	
	3rd - 14th		A Pioneer Course of 3 Officers & 36 men from 3rd Cav. Bde. was held at DOURIEZ under Lt. S.J. ARMSTRONG. Training & drills both mounted & dismounted were carried on throughout the month. An instructor was obtained from St. Pancras to teach Riding School.	

R. Armstrong
Major R.E.
OC 2nd Fd. Sqdn.

CONFIDENTIAL.

Vol 28

WAR   DIARY

of

2nd FIELD SQUADRON, R.E.

JANUARY, 1917

VOL. XXIX.

Army Form C. 2118

WAR DIARY
INTELLIGENCE SUMMARY
(Erase heading not required.)

Place	Date	Hour	Summary of Events and Information	Remarks and references to Appendices
PONCHES-ESTRUVAL	January 1917 1st-15th		Syke remained in the field the whole month. Continued work on improving fields for aviation.  Lt. ARMSTRONG & 10 O.R. worked on home defs at AUCHY-LEZ-HESDIN. Owing to have no 2 Brigades in their area, this work was stopped.	
	2nd-10th		Major SWINBURNE attended course at R.E. School of Instruction LE PARCQUE.	
	14th-25th		Pioneer Course of 3 Officers & 36 O.R. of 5th Cav. Bde. was carried out.	
	8th-27th		Lt THOMAS & 18 O.R. was attached to 4th Cav. Pioneer Battn. 2nd Lt KEZAR & 18 O.R. " - " - " - 3 " - " - Both parties were on railway work, doubling existing line, & were at SAVY – Later at MAZINGARBE. They were employed on earth work & platelaying. On 27th both the Officers were withdrawn & the parties reduced from 18 to 12 O.R. each.	
	29th		Lt FORSYTH & WAGHORN with 30 O.R. were sent on with Cavalry Divisional party to prepare new Hutting Area for 5th Cav. Bde.	

Signature
J.H. Swinburne
Major
O.C. 2nd Cav. Sqdn.

CONFIDENTIAL.

WAR   DIARY

of

2nd FIELD SQUADRON, R.E.

FEBRUARY, 1917.
VOL. XXX.

============

Army Form C. 2118

Instructions regarding War Diaries and Intelligence Summaries are contained in F. S. Regs., Part II. and the Staff Manual respectively. Title Pages will be prepared in manuscript.

WAR DIARY

INTELLIGENCE SUMMARY

(Erase heading not required.)

2nd Field Squadron R.E.

Place	Date	Hour	Summary of Events and Information	Remarks and references to Appendices
PONCHES - ESTRUVAL				
February 1917.				
	1st	19h	Squadron remained in billets throughout the month, 26 O.R. being attached to Cavalry Pioneer Battn.	
	2nd	12.5	2 officers + 30 O.R. were engaged getting 5th Cav Bde into new trench area.	
	18th - 28th		Capt WISE MC RE attended a course in heavy bridging at AIRE. Lt ARMSTRONG RE attended a course at Rittoval School.	
	5th		Bridging detachment left to join Corps Bridging Train.	
	23rd		Reinforcement of 20 dismounted sappers joined — to be held surplus to establishment.	
	25th		Lt THOMAS + 2/Lt KEZAR + 29 O.R. went out to prepare new trench area for 4 Cav. Bde.	

A. Wise Capt. R.E.
for O.C. 2nd Field Squadron R.E.

1875 Wt. W593/826 1,000,000 4/15 J.B.C. & A. A.D.S.S./Forms/C. 2118.

CONFIDENTIAL.

WAR   DIARY

of

2nd FIELD SQUADRON, R.E.

MARCH, 1917.

VOL. XXXI.

WAR DIARY

INTELLIGENCE SUMMARY

Army Form C. 2118

Place	Date	Hour	Summary of Events and Information	Remarks and references to Appendices
PERONNE	March 1917. 13-15th		Squadron Numbers filled throughout the month. Squadron Training was carried on as far as possible.	
	15th		Detachment from Brigwy Train now available for pontier with field Park Equipment.	
	3rd		Detachment of 3rd + 5th Pioneer Battn rejoined.	
			Lt Keghorn & 31 O.R. proceeded on detachment to BAILLEULMONT to Corps with water supply.	
	19th		Lt F.G. Thorn to hospital sick.	
	8th-19th		Pioneer Course for 45 Brigade to be held.	
	23rd-31st		Lt Kezar & 23 O.R. been on detachment near ARRAS in connection with Cavalry Tracks.	
	30th		Lt Keghorn returned to Squadron.	
	31st		Lt A.W. Sproule joined Squadron from Base.	

2/4/17

CONFIDENTIAL.

WAR   DIARY

of

2nd FIELD SQUADRON, R.E.

APRIL, 1917.

VOL. XXXII.

WAR DIARY
INTELLIGENCE SUMMARY

Army Form C. 2118

Place	Date	Hour	Summary of Events and Information	Remarks and references to Appendices
PONCHES ESTRUVAL	APRIL 1917 1st–8th		Inactive.	
		7ᵃᵐ	Marched complete to BEAUVOIS-RIVIERE to HDQRS.	
	8.			
	9ᵗʰ	9 am	1st portion of Regiment — ROTTUIE sent out detmt of B Sqn's	
			hostile up to 2pm " " " just west of HARP. No 1 Troop
		2pm.	accompanied 3rd Car Bde — No 2 Troop — 5th Car Bde — No 3 — 4 Car Bde
			A Echelon Bivouacked. B Echelon in Sub-Corps area.
		5pm.	3rd / 5th Bns (not forward) PARAS HANCOURT + atry
			THILLOY — HANCOURT road respectively.
			2nd portion Regiment. No troops sent out through heavy MG
			obtained party (supplied Cavalry track
			from A Echelon battery to take in AGNY
		9pm.	to WALLY. Hostile 2 am Bivouacked. No 1 Field Agny.
	10.	2pm	Advanced to same positions from which the batteries yesterday.
			No 1, No 3 (forward) in ROTTUIE. No 2 forwarded when
			East of THILLOY.
	11.	6 am	Took up same positions from which the batteries yesterday.

Army Form C. 2118

WAR DIARY
INTELLIGENCE SUMMARY
(Erase heading not required.)

Instructions regarding War Diaries and Intelligence Summaries are contained in F. S. Regs., Part II. and the Staff Manual respectively. Title Pages will be prepared in manuscript.

Place	Date	Hour	Summary of Events and Information	Remarks and references to Appendices
	11th April 1917.	12 noon	Withdrew Nos 1 & 2 Troops from Brigade Concentrates for Reserve Bde.	
		2pm	Withdrew 6 bullets AGNY.	
AGNY.	12.IV	2pm	Marched back to previous Bdes. HdQrs	
HENU	13.IV.30		Remained in H.Q. Work has been deficiency Cavalry Wales Roundup in Pas area.	
	21st		Sapper RODWAY awarded Military Medal at Corps Ceremony the Troop Lieuts having incorrectly left behind on the left of R. 10.R. U.F. RIDGE returning to join his Troop tried to & believing in this he succeeded, in pursuit turning horsey to tender horses to take no fall over to enemy trenches upon shelling.	

13/17

WAR-DIARY
of
2nd Field Squadron.
R.-E.
From 1.5.17 to 31.5.17

VOLUME XXXIII

WAR DIARY
or
INTELLIGENCE SUMMARY
(Erase heading not required.)

Army Form C. 2118

Place	Date	Hour	Summary of Events and Information	Remarks and references to Appendices
MENU	May 1st	8:15	Infilled. Work was carried on with improvement of stables to	
		9:15	marched to MEAULT via FORCEVILLE, being handed over to 78th Corps.	
		10:15	" " DOIGNT - PERONNE	
		11:15	" " MARQUAIX. Reconnoitred for horse water points	
		12:15 — 14:15	looked on water points — Reconnoitred 42nd Div line which he are taking over line consists of a series of posts for about 100 men each. There are 12 such on a front of 7000 yds. These are wire, barb in places, all along the front. Posts in left sector are wired round. Nothing on Right sector. Divisional boundaries are line F.30.a.50 - L4a.97 - K.11.c.22 x18C95. x16a.18. W30a.81. System consists of an outpost line (Green Line - Brown +E.5a.32.81. Line. Former is very weak, small isolated points of trench held by sections of 4 sections. Lines to communication back to Green line. Elements F.W. & Birdcage are the only 2 advanced posts held in Aprey sh, about 4 plan each. They are 600' in front of Green line. Green line runs along high ground from Post 7 F29 6 24, through TOMBON & little PRIEL FARMS to Post N. x21 6 99. This line is at present	

WAR DIARY
or
INTELLIGENCE SUMMARY

Army Form C. 2118

(Erase heading not required.)

Place	Date	Hour	Summary of Events and Information	Remarks and references to Appendices
	15th		Line of Rawlins. At an average distance of 800x behind Green Line is Brown line from F22d.14 in front of Ronssoy, & EPEHY to F.1.a. This line is heavily wired but to thin work has been done on it. RE at my disposal is CRE. 2nd & 3rd Sections of 108th Tunnelling Coy. under Capt Brown Laycock, latter au at pres. Sent employed on wells.	
	16th		Lieut. Temp Capt A.V.D.Byles M.C. RE killed in boat E. in Ronssoy	
	17th		2nd Tr Tyler moved into billets in Ronssoy	
	19th		3rd Tr Tyler — EPEHY	
	20th 24th		Took over line from CRE 42nd Div - Col MOSELY RE - at 9 am. Worked on improvement of Green line posts, dugouts for Regl HQ. & Brewery etc. Cleaned out of wells. Major Simoto M.C. R.E. with 2/1st & 2/1st B Sherwood Foresters, worked in town of Brown line. Capt COBB MC RE took over RE dumps at S. EMILIE.	
	25th		3rd Car Div took over sept Sector from 3rd Car Bde. Army disposal from this date. 2nd Tr Tyler - No. 1 Section 108th Tunnelling Coy.	
	25th-31st		Work continued on Green line posts - improved defences &	

WAR DIARY
or
INTELLIGENCE SUMMARY

Army Form C. 2118

(Erase heading not required.)

Place	Date	Hour	Summary of Events and Information	Remarks and references to Appendices
	25th-	31st	& Communication to Gillemont Farm. 2/8 Sherwood Foresters & 2/5- N. Stafford lines posts protected & Barbed Wire. Work was begun on Post forming a switch from Little PRIEL Fm to	
LEMPIRE.			180 Rly were employed on wells & on mined dug out for Bde. Hd. Regt - H.Q.	
	24th		N° 107745 Sapper DOUGLASS. RE. 2nd 75 Tyh reported missing.	

Thornborne
Major
OC 2 an Fd Sqn.
of CRE 2nd Can Div

3/6/17.

CONFIDENTIAL
WAR - DIARY
OF
2nd FIELD SQDN R.E.
FROM 1.6.17. TO 30.6.17.
(VOLUME 34)

Army Form C. 2118

Instructions regarding War Diaries and Intelligence Summaries are contained in F.S. Regs., Part II. and the Staff Manual respectively. Title Pages will be prepared in manuscript.

WAR DIARY
or
INTELLIGENCE SUMMARY
(Erase heading not required.)

Place	Date	Hour	Summary of Events and Information	Remarks and references to Appendices
ROISEL.	June 1917 1st – 8th		Carried on work on Outpost Intermediate line including Switch from Little Priel Fm to Templeux. Pots Avre Avg, Frontages trench-boarded — sandbags, Dug-outs - wire. All wired & intermediate & support sandbags, dumps - wire strengthened & strengthened where necessary. wire added where lacking & strengthened where necessary.	
		9th	Raid was carried out on German trenches East of Gillemont Fm. Capt Armstrong & 15 O.R. were prepared with charges both for Gappay, both wire & demolishing enemy dugouts. No opportunity to found for any the Sappers but Capt Armstrong made a useful reconnaissance of the burrowing underground portions of the farm buildings & enclosures. A charge was carried in the German line heads (concealed) brought back to our trench to await a suitable occasion for firing.	
		13th	No 33114 Sapper STREET awarded Military Medal by Corps Commander for gallantry on night of 9/5 in bringing in wounded.	
		16th	Capt ARMSTRONG S.J. R.E. awarded Military Cross for	

1875 Wt. W593/826 1,000,000 4/15 J.B.C. & A. A.D.S.S./Forms/C. 2118.

Army Form C. 2118

WAR DIARY
or
INTELLIGENCE SUMMARY
(Erase heading not required.)

Instructions regarding War Diaries and Intelligence Summaries are contained in F.S. Regs., Part II. and the Staff Manual respectively. Title Pages will be prepared in manuscript.

Place	Date	Hour	Summary of Events and Information	Remarks and references to Appendices
June	1917 21st	16.15 22.00	Gallantry & good work on night of 9th inst. The gunners to Lieut Gillemont for fathers attending party were covering from wiring.	
	22nd		No. 25499 Sapper SLATER R.E. killed	
	29th		Took over line to our North from 3rd Cav. Div. Our divisional front is therefore the same as it was on 19.5.17. Chestwork taken by 3 Cav Div. to two long Coals trenches. one from post R. 15 to 15 Bis stage, the other from R.2. H.Q. post post 15 left Outpost H.Q.	
	1st – 30th		Usual work on line Carried on. 10th Coy employing on deep command posts in every post at Gillemont. Baths installed at S. Emilie turning on 29.6.17	
	1st		Lt. THOMAS F.S. rejoined from Base.	

T.A.Osbourne Major
OC 2nd/1st W.Ldn.
OC 2[?]

30/6/17

Vol 34
27.7.17

CONFIDENTIAL

WAR - DIARY

OF

2nd FIELD. SQUADRON R.E.

FROM 1.7.17. — To 31. 7. 17

(VOLUME - 35.)

WAR DIARY
INTELLIGENCE SUMMARY

Army Form C. 2118

(Erase heading not required.)

Instructions regarding War Diaries and Intelligence Summaries are contained in F.S. Regs., Part II. and the Staff Manual respectively. Title Pages will be prepared in manuscript.

Place	Date	Hour	Summary of Events and Information	Remarks and references to Appendices
ROISEL	July 1917 1st–6th		Carried on work on Outpost and Intermediate Line including Switch from Little PRIEL Fm to L'EMPIRE.	
	3rd/4th		A raid on a small scale was carried on the German Trenches East of GILLEMONT Fm. 2 Patrols of the Oxford Hussars entered the enemy's trenches. 2 Sappers accompanied each patrol and successfully cut the enemy wire with Bangalore torpedoes.	
	4th		No. 133482 Sapper HOUSTON R.E. wounded and evacuated.	
	6th.		Major T.A. Swinburne D.S.O. R.E. handed over the line to CRE 35th Division. Handed over Right Sector to 203rd Field Coy. R.E. Major SEMPLE R.E.	
MARQUAIX	6th/7th		2nd Fld. Sqdn. moved back to horse lines at MARQUAIX.	
	9th		Marched to BUIRE	
	13th		Marched to SUZANNE via CLERY-sur-SOMME	
	14th		Marched to VILLE-SOUS-CORBIE	
	15th		Marched to AUTHIE	
	16th		Marched to MAGNICOURT.	
MAGNICOURT	17th–31st		In Billets at MAGNICOURT. Improved Water Supply of Divisional Area. Improved Cavalry Corps Depot Camp at FRÉVENT	

31/7/17.   S.T. Annesley Capt. R.E.
for O.C. 2nd Fd. Sqdn.

Vol 35

CONFIDENTIAL.
WAR DIARY
of
2nd Field Squadron RE
from 1.8.17 to 31.8.17.
(Volume - 36)

WAR DIARY
or
INTELLIGENCE SUMMARY

(Erase heading not required.)

Instructions regarding War Diaries and Intelligence Summaries are contained in F.S. Regs., Part II. and the Staff Manual respectively. Title Pages will be prepared in manuscript.

Place	Date	Hour	Summary of Events and Information	Remarks and references to Appendices
MAENICOURT SUR CANCHE.	August 1-31st		Squadron remained in billets throughout the month. Training in Musketry & Rapid Bridging was carried out. Completion of the Cav Corps Depôt Camp at FREVENT about the 15-16 was followed by its immediate abandonment therefrom.	
	14th		Lt. F.G. THOMAS R.E. left Sqdn to join 23rd Field Company.	

J. Moncrieffe
Major R.E.
O.C. 2nd Fd Sqn

CONFIDENTIAL

WAR DIARY OF

2nd FIELD SQUADRON. R.E.

FROM :- 1.9.17 — TO — 30.9.17.

VOLUME - Nº :- 37.

WAR DIARY
or
INTELLIGENCE SUMMARY

Army Form C. 2118

Place	Date	Hour	Summary of Events and Information	Remarks and references to Appendices
MAGNICOURT.	Sep. 1 – 4th	—	Remained in billets	
	5th	—	Moved to MONCHEAUX & MONTS-EN-TERNOIS	
	13th	—	Lt FORSYTH & 14 O.R. went up to join 3rd Bde R.H.Q. near LENS to assist in manufacture of O.P's, dug-outs etc.	
	16th	2nd Lt WARREN & 25 O.R. joined 4th to assist in construction of electric lighting etc in ATHIES area.	
	24th	Lt WAGHORN & 21 O.R. reported on visit from III Army Infy School at PON-LS-CHATEAU where they had been erecting huts.	
			Throughout the month training of N.C.O's & men was carried on as far as possible with from 30 to 80 O.R. absent. Particular attention was paid to the construction of all kinds in the 4 standard patterns of wire entanglements both by day & night.	

J. Troubridge
Major R.E.
O.C. 2nd [Field Coy]

Vol 37

CONFIDENTIAL

WAR - DIARY
of
2nd FIELD-SQUADRON-RE
FROM 1.10.17 to 31.10.17

VOLUME NUMBER NO - 38.

WAR DIARY or INTELLIGENCE SUMMARY

Army Form C. 2118

(Erase heading not required.)

Place	Date	Hour	Summary of Events and Information	Remarks and references to Appendices
	October 1	7k	Billets at MONCHEAUX & MONTS EN TERNOIS. Lt Forsyth Party reported on Oct 3rd	
		8th	Marched to TANGRY	
		10th	" SAINS-LEZ-PERNES	
		17th	" SERICOURT	
		19th	" ST HILAIRE	
		20th	" CORBIE	
		21st	" BRUSLE	
	22nd - 31st		Whole Squadron employed on trailer hutting & battery & dug outs in CORBIGNY area. Took over a Cavalry working party of about 800 men. Twelve hunghuts all efforts were concentrated on providing cover for men & horses.	
	24th		Lt Alexander + 25 OR joined from 1st to 4th for work.	
	31st		Lt Hay + 2nd Lt Balfa + 35 OR " "	
			Throughout the month 2nd harveen & party were employed in hutting in 4th Cav Bde Area. 27 Cavalry are attached to spec to look after horses	

Vol 38

Confidential
War Diary of
2nd Field Squadron R.E.
From 1.11.17 to 30-11-17
Volume No — 29.

WAR DIARY
or
INTELLIGENCE SUMMARY

(Erase heading not required.)

Army Form C. 2118

Place	Date	Hour	Summary of Events and Information	Remarks and references to Appendices
BRUSLE	Nov. 1-9th		Halting was continued in CARTIGNY area.	
	10th		Lt ALEXANDER + his party joined 3rd Hussars at BOISGNY + Lt MATHEWSON.RE + 18 O.R. 5th L.D. joined this unit.	
		12^K	Lt MATHEWSON's party joined 5th L.D. at BRAS. F.N. 2nd Field Sqdn	
	13th 18th		moved to TERTRY where 2nd Lt WARREN's party rejoined. Continued halting in TERTRY area.	
	20th	2 a.m. 4 p.m.	Marches (less B. echelon) to VILLERS-FAUCON area.	
		12.15 p.m.	Advanced by Cavalry Track to Boulton just south of NASNIERES. One Troop was attached to each Brigade. The following Special parties were All'n rendezvous.	
			a) 1 Lt. 4 O.R. + 3 packs blockers work special Edu of 2nd Dragoons 15 triton, was to cut the BUSIGNY - CAMBRAI Railway to far East as possible.	
			b) 1 Officer (4 R.S. VAGHORN RE) 10 O.R. + 6 packs. E took H.Car Bde. 15 Hussars was to destroy the Bridge at NEUVILLE sur ESCAUT & to prepare for demolition the Bridges in the vicinity of BOUCHAIN	
			Field Sqdn. Commander was with G.O.C. Division. 2nd in Command was with Troops in Divisional Reserve.	

Army Form C. 2118.

WAR DIARY
or
INTELLIGENCE SUMMARY
(Erase heading not required.)

Instructions regarding War Diaries and Intelligence Summaries are contained in F.S. Regs, Part II. and the Staff Manual respectively. Title Pages will be prepared in manuscript.

Place	Date	Hour	Summary of Events and Information	Remarks and references to Appendices
	21st	4 p.m.	Returned to VILLERS-FAUCON area where 4th Bde was concentrated	
	22nd		Remained in same area	
	23rd	4.15 p.m.	Marched to EQUANCOURT area. Bivouac'd in BIVOUAC RUE.	
	24th	2 p.m.	" " DESSART WOOD.	
DESSART WOOD	25th	6.15 a.m.	Marched to RIBECOURT area, the hoof being again attacked to each Brigade for active operations.	
		3.30 p.m.	Returned to DESSART WOOD. Casualties 1 O.R. wounded	
	26th – 29th		Remained in same area	
	30th		Marched for BRAS FARM but unit ordered while en route owing to severe German attack. Bivouac'd at DESSART WOOD. B. Echelon rejoined unit at DESSART WOOD on 28th & later to BRAS FARM on the 30th when they returned together to the wounded men	

Signed
R. Stewart
Major
O.C. 2nd Squadron

1875 Wt. W593/826 1,000,000 4/15 J.B.C. & A. A.D.S.S./Forms/C. 2118.

Confidential

War — Diary
of
2nd Field Squadron RE.
From 1.12.17 to 31.12.17

VOL XL

Army Form C. 2118

WAR DIARY or INTELLIGENCE SUMMARY
(Erase heading not required.)

Place	Date	Hour	Summary of Events and Information	Remarks and references to Appendices
DESSART WOOD (FINS)	Dec 1st		Working Party of 1000 Cav employed by Major Jeffery moving subsoil West of GOUZEAUCOURT from Q.35. central to W.S.d.3.1. left was in touch with GDs div + Right with 1st Cav Bde. who were also employed in continuation of this line. A Sqdn was employed chiefly on wire + supervision.	
	2nd + 3rd		This work was continued + a similar line constructed from W.S.d.32 back to old Brown line just N.E. of REVELON Fm.	
	4th		1 Troop + 30 Cav. wired 300x of front line from VAUCELETTE Farm. 1 Sect RE + 100 Cav dug support trench westn end of GAUCHE WOOD northwards	
	5th 6th		1 Troop continued work on support line, trench commenced on 3rd Dr came out of line.	
	7th		Squadron marched to BUS FARM	
	8th		" " LAMOTTE - BREBIERE	
			" " NAMPTY. South of AMIENS.	
NAMPTY	9th — 18th		Rested + Refitted at NAMPTY	
	19th		Marched to SAUSEUX, entrained 6.30am, detrained ROUEL 12 noon, marched to MONTIGNY. Strength 5 Officers 87 O.R. including 6 O.R. In 11th Lancers, the	
			Handed by on 17th, arriving MONTIGNY on 20th.	
			Moved HQ camp to HERVILLY. 2 Officers + 2 hoops (No 1 + 2) Zy ones	
HERVILLY	21.		1st Aug into in L.10.a. Major SWINBURNE took over R.E. charge	

WAR DIARY
or
INTELLIGENCE SUMMARY

Army Form C. 2118

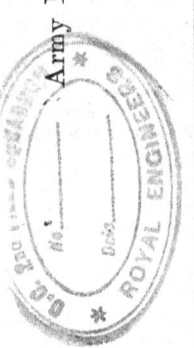

Place	Date	Hour	Summary of Events and Information	Remarks and references to Appendices
HERVILLY	21st		Of the Centre Sector from Capt GREATHEAD RE 1639 Fd.Coy. Boundaries at present TURNIP LANE on the North & CLUB TRACK on the South (Inclusive) now on Defence of HILLCREST. Who shewing Keenness for same. Right boundary extended to include N°6 post. Casualties. 1 OR Killed. 3 OR wounded.	
	22nd 25th			
	26th			
	27th - 31st		(Sat) CLUB TR. MER TR. Railway puppet & post of HILLCREST. Lt. J.S FORSYTH attended a course at Heavy Bridging School AIRE. Commencing 20 Inst. 2 NCOs attended Course at Divisional School from 10th to 22nd. HQ horses returned at NAMPTY	

M. Lawrence Re.
Major RE.
OC 2nd wto Bgn.

Confidential

War Diary of
No. 4a Squadron R.E.
From 1.1.18 to 31.1.18.

Volume No 41.

WAR DIARY
or
INTELLIGENCE SUMMARY
(Erase heading not required.)

Army Form C. 2118

Instructions regarding War Diaries and Intelligence Summaries are contained in F.S. Regs., Part II. and the Staff Manual respectively. Title Pages will be prepared in manuscript.

Place	Date	Hour	Summary of Events and Information	Remarks and references to Appendices
HERVILLY	January 1st – 16th		Work continued in Centre Sector, chiefly in TURNIP LANE - HILLCREST - CLUB Tr + Post- HILLCREST defences + PRIEL ROAD per. Hard frost followed by sudden thaw caused complete collapse of most of trenches + rendered them in many places impassable.	
	17th		Lt. G.L. KEZAR, Cpl. A. GUY & DCM Lce Cpl. LIDDINGTON & Spr GUNN accompanied raid by 6th Bn. Q. They cut enemy's wire, entered the trench, captured a German sentry.	
	18th		Statutory tour.	
	21st		Work continued.	
	22nd		Capt. GUY awarded M. Libary Medal by Corps Commander for his work in connection with raid.	
	18th		Lt. V.E. de MERIC, T.F.R.E. joined Siber.	
	27th		Lt. A.W. SPROULL S.R. RE left unit to join No 24 Anti-Aircraft Search.	
	31st		L.H. Sector. Work continued.	
	13th		Sgt. J.R.O.BISAR. SEM & Corp! POTTER attended Divisional Equitation Course School.	
	16th		Lt. R.S. WAGHORN + Sgt. ALDERSON " " "	
23rd	6th		S.M. C P LOVELL joined unit as S.S.M. Vice RSM. H.W. TAYLOR evacuated sick.	
			Throughout the month Capt S.J. ARMSTRONG M.C. R.E. officiated as Staff Officer in office of C.R.E. Car Corps. H.Q. remained at NAMPTY the whole month.	

T. Kinburne
Major
CRE 2nd Corps

Vol 41

R.S.10
287/18

Confidential

War Diary of
No 2 Field Squadron R.E.
From 1.2.18   28.2.18

Volume No 42

WAR DIARY or INTELLIGENCE SUMMARY

Army Form C. 2118

Sem/1918

Place	Date	Hour	Summary of Events and Information	Remarks and references to Appendices
February. Hervilly.	1st – 13th		Work was continued on Four Line drainage – Wheat defences – Annual Fence connecting S. posts – Club Trench to Blain has received orders to proceed – 8tv which had relieved 2nd Div Bty on 29th ult. Lieut R.L Regan reported Wilking Coy for his work on road. on 17.1.18. H.Q. of Bn moved from MAMPTY to HARBONNIÈRES.	
	7th		" HARBONNIÈRES to Camp near SOHM.	
	8th		" " "	
Fourques	14th		" to FOURQUES " H.R. 70 Gen Camp	
			Advanced party relieved by 163rd Fd Coy in the line & marched to FOURQUES to join remainder.	
	16th		Lieut J.S FORSYTH & Sgt PRICE proceeded to Allied Divisional School	
			Cpl. GUY – DURERS + HARDWICK – Equitation Course	
			Lieut R. STAGHORN – Cpl. DAY – Cpl McKENZIE attended Belgian Croix de Guerre	
	9th		Lieut FORSYTH gazetted T/Capt	
			NAGHORN " Capt. Auto Gunnery 6 3.11.17.	
	17th – 23rd		Bn deft.ed at FOURQUES & did a little necessary leading in Divisional Area	
	23rd – 28th		Bridges on ATHIES – TERRY – ST CHRIST area prepared for demolition.	

J.T. Amstrong
Capt. RE
to O.C. 2nd Field Sqn.

WAR DIARY
or
INTELLIGENCE SUMMARY

(Erase heading not required.)

Army Form C. 2118

March 1918

Place	Date	Hour	Summary of Events and Information	Remarks and references to Appendices
March. FOURQUES	1st – 7th			
"	1st	3rd	Bridges in the ATHIES, TERTRY & ST CHRIST AREA prepared for demolition and handed over to 258 Tun. Coy RE & 288 A.T. Coy. RE	
"	4th – 7th		Preparation for the accommodation of 4000 men in tear fos" in ATHIES & MONCHY LAGACHE	
VIERMAND	7th		Dismounted Field Sqdn. formed and take over VADENCOURT - MAISSEMY Sector to 4th Field Sqdn. Led horses	
"	7th – 11th		No 1 Troop at MAISSEMY worked in front line defences and ESSLING REDOUBT, No 3 " at VADENCOURT " " " VADENCOURT Defences No 2 " at VIERMAND " Hauling & preparation of bridges to demolitions	
"	10.		T/Captain FORSYTH left to join 4th Field Squadron	
FOURQUES	11th		Dis.d Field Sqdn. returned to FOURQUES. Work was handed over to 103rd Field Coy. RE	
"	11th – 13th			
MAUCOURT	13th		Sqdn. marched to MAUCOURT. bivouacked in Wood.	
"	13th		19 Lieut. A.H.LLOYD, M.C. R.E. joined Sqdn. from the 4th Field Squadron.	
"	14th – 18th		Sqdn. worked on water points for the Division.	
"	20th	22	" prepared bridges over OISE & Canal for demolition	
"	21st		3 Troops left dismounted & joined dismounted Brigades, who went up in Busses to support the Infantry	
"	21st – 23rd		No 1. Troop gallantly defended post at JUSSY under Lieut KEZAR. M.C R.E. Nos 2 & 3. worked in defences to their Bvec. H.Q. Dismounted party under Capt. ARMSTRONG, prepared bridges over R. Oise & Canal for Demolition. No 1 lost 10 O.R. Killed Wounded & missing	

WAR DIARY or INTELLIGENCE SUMMARY

Army Form C. 2118

Place	Date	Hour	Summary of Events and Information	Remarks and references to Appendices
March	23		No. 1 & No. 2 Troops rejoined Sqdn.	
PONTOISE	"		Sqdn. moved to PONTOISE	
BAILLY	24.		" " BAILLY.	
"	25.		H.Q. Dis'd Party blew up bridges at APPILLY & BRETIGNY in orders of French and then rejoined Sqdn. at BAILLY.	
			Mounted Sqdn. under Major SWINBURNE. D.S.O. moved to PONTOISE.	
	25		and prepared and destroyed bridges at PONTOISE over canal & R. OISE.	
Nupt.	25 & 26.		H.Q. Sqdn. & transport moved to neighbourhood of COMPIEGNE.	
	26.		" " " " " West "	
	27.		" " " to VONQUIERES. No 3. Troop rejoined.	
	26.		Action at DIVE LE FRANC & CHIRY. Sqdn. prepared & blew bridges.	
JONQUIÈRES	27		Mounted Sqdn. moved to JONQUIÈRES & rejoined H.Q.	
AUSAUVILLERS	28		Sqdn. moved to AUSAUVILLERS. (during the day 28" Troops were attached to Rein. bdes.)	
"	29		Troops moved up to assist in preparing defence of BOVES, PLAINVILLERS & WELLES.	
BOVES	29		Sqdn. moved to BOVES	
"	30		Sqdn. moved out to Bois de BLANGY and returned in the evening to BOVES	
"	31		Sqdn. moved out to Bois de GENTELLES and worked on defences SE of th' Wood on DOMART ROAD. and returned at' Bois de GENTELLES	

J. Armitage Capt. R.E.
O/c. 2nd FIELD SQDN., R.E.

Confidential

War Diary
of
2nd Field Squadron R.E.
from 1.4.18. to 30.4.18.
Volume No 44

Army Form C. 2118

WAR DIARY
or
INTELLIGENCE SUMMARY

of 2nd FIELD SQUADRON ROYAL ENGINEERS

(Erase heading not required.)

Instructions regarding War Diaries and Intelligence Summaries are contained in F.S. Regs., Part II. and the Staff Manual respectively. Title Pages will be prepared in manuscript.

Place	Date	Hour	Summary of Events and Information	Remarks and references to Appendices
BOVES	APRIL 1st	4.45 am	Squadron marched from BOIS DE GENTELLES to position of readiness near HOURGES. The led horses was then sent back to the BOIS DE GENTELLES.	
	"	9.0 am	2nd Cavalry Division counter attacked and retook wood 1 mile S. of HANGARD. 4th Field Sqdn. assisted the consolidation of the position regained, the 3 Troops digging posts in the edge of the wood and to the westward of it. Major T.A. SWINBURNE D.S.O., R.E. killed and Lieut de MARIC R.E. slightly wounded. 10 R killed + 30 R wounded.	
	"	3 pm	Sqdn. returned to the BOIS DE GENTELLES.	
	"	5 pm	Sqdn. returned to BOVES.	
RIVERY	3rd		Sqdn. moved to RIVERY. B. Echelon rejoined.	
	4th		Lt. MacDOWALL R.E.(T) + 18 O.R. joined Sqdn. as reinforcement for 4th Field Sqdn. R.E.	
FAMECHON	6th	6 am	Sqdn. moved to FAMECHON (Near AILLY).	
	6th – 10th		Sqdn. rested and refitted.	
	9th		Lt CHANCE R.E. joined Sqdn. from 5th Field Sqdn. R.E.	
AUXI-LE-CHATEAU	10th	3 pm	Sqdn. moved to AUXI-LE-CHATEAU. "B" Echelon + Dis? han to FAUCOURT.	
PETIGNY	12th	3 pm	" " PETIGNY near ROMY. Lorry refilled with tools and joined M.T. Coy, ASC.	
BLARINGHEM	13th	2.30 pm	" " BLARINGHEM. + billeted at farm 1/2 mile N of village.	
	15th – 16th		Defuge system E to NE of MORBECQUE on being ? to CRE 1st Australian Divn.	
	19th		Lorry rejoined. "B" Echelon	
	20th		Sqdn. worked in BOIS DES VACHES on making huddles + pickets for CRE. 29th Divn.	
	21st	24 B	" " " Defures system near le TIR ANGLAIS. in being for CRE 29th Div.	
	21st – 28th		1 Sec. 200 R. " " " Training was carried on during this period. N.Cos instructed in Hotchkiss Guns.	
COYECQUE	29th		Troop training and dismounted fire action also fire observation also judging distances etc.	
	30th		Sqdn. moved to COYECQUE + billeted in village to jour L mile NE of village.	

Sapper WHITE awarded Military Medal.

Lieut: G.L. KEZAR MC R.E. awarded Bar to his M.C. for his gallantry behaviour at JUSSY on 23.3.18.

Sapper W.H. WALKER RAMC (attached Military Cross for gallant conduct O/o 2nd FIELD SQDN. R.E. for gallant conduct at Div. HQ. LE FRANC on 26.3.18

P.T. Armstrong
Major RE

1875 Wt. W 826 1,000,000 4/15 J.B.C. & A. A.D.S.S./Forms/C. 2118.

Confidential

War Diary
of
No 7 Fleet Spotters R.S.
from 1.5.18 to 31.5.18

Volume Nº. 45.

Army Form C. 2118

WAR DIARY
or
INTELLIGENCE SUMMARY of 2nd FIELD SQUADRON ROYAL ENGINEERS

(Erase heading not required.)

Instructions regarding War Diaries and Intelligence Summaries are contained in F.S. Regs., Part II. and the Staff Manual respectively. Title Pages will be prepared in manuscript.

Place	Date	Hour	Summary of Events and Information	Remarks and references to Appendices
COYECQUE	MAY 1st	—	Sqdn billeted in farm ½ East of COYECQUE.	
LE MARAIS	2nd	—	" marched to LE MARAIS near FRUGES and billeted.	
"	3rd-4th	—	" billeted at LE MARAIS. Workshop started for manufacture of chaff-cutters.	
ALETTE	5th	—	" marched to ALETTE and billeted.	
"	6th-19th	—	" billeted at ALETTE. Workshop established for manufacture of chaff-cutters. Musketry, signalling, riding, driving, troop & squadron training carried out.	
FROIDVAL	20th	—	Sqdn. placed under 1st Army for work under X Corps. Sqdn. marched to FROIDVAL, 3 miles West of ANVIN. Small detachment left at ALETTE.	Sheet 44.B. J 26 d. 4.2.
VIELFORT	21st	—	Sqdn. marched to VIELFORT. 1 mile N. of HOUDAIN.	
"	22nd -31st	—	Sqdn. employed on No 3 Sub Section B.B. line on supervision of infantry working parties and assistance in technical work with Lt Col NAPIER-CLAVERING DSO R.E. C.R.E. A Sector. B.B. line.	

J. Armstrong
Major R.E.
O/c. 2nd FIELD SQDN, R.E.

Confidential

War Diary
of
2nd Field Squadron R.E.
From 1/6/18 to 30/6/18

Volume No. 46

Army Form C. 2118

WAR DIARY

INTELLIGENCE SUMMARY

of 2nd Field Squadron Royal Engineers

(Erase heading not required.)

Place	Date	Hour	Summary of Events and Information	Remarks and references to Appendices
	JUNE			
VIELFORT	1st –30		Sqdn. was employed under the X Corps in supervision of Infantry and Chinese working parties and as Technical assistance on No 2 Subsector. B.B. line.	
[CAYEUX]	17th–24th 24th 30		Lieut G. L KEZAR MC RE attended course at Cavalry Corps Gas School.	
"	17th		Lieut K.M MACDOWELL RE " " " " Gasification "	
			Farrier Staff Sergeant. SPACKMAN awarded the Meritorious Service Medal. (MSM)	
			Cpl WINDOWSON " " " " " (Killed 1.4.18)	
			Captain J S FORSYTH. RE (Transferred to 4th Fld Sqdn. 3.18) Mentioned in despatches.	

P. J. Armstrong
Major RE
OC 2nd Field Sqdn RE

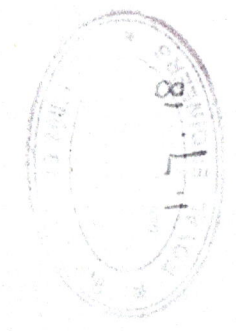

Vol 46

CONFIDENTIAL

WAR – DIARY
of
2nd FIELD SQUADRON RE
FROM
1.7.18 to 31.7.18

Volume No 47.

Army Form C. 2118

WAR DIARY
or
INTELLIGENCE SUMMARY

2nd FIELD SQUADRON R.E.

(Erase heading not required.)

Instructions regarding War Diaries and Intelligence Summaries are contained in F.S. Regs., Part II. and the Staff Manual respectively. Title Pages will be prepared in manuscript.

Place	Date	Hour	Summary of Events and Information	Remarks and references to Appendices
	JULY			
VIELFORT (near HOUDAIN)	1st – 10th		Squadron employed by 1st Army on G.H.Q. defence near BRUAY. Work on B.R. line under X Corps. consisting of supervision of Chinese Labour, technical work in draining, wiring and revetments.	
FRAMECOURT	10th		Marched to FRAMECOURT.	
WILLENCOURT (VIELFORT)	11th		Marched to WILLENCOURT near AUXI-LE-CHATEAU & att'd to Cav. Corps & bridging.	
WILLENCOURT	9th		2/Lt C.F. TURNER joined the unit from the Base.	
"	12th		Bridging Practice with Cav. Steel Boat Equipment.	
"	13th		Lt KEZAR McR.E. left the unit for England for duty in INDIA	
SARS-LEZ-BOIS	15th		Sqdn. marched to SARS-LEZ-BOIS & rejoined Division.	
"	15th – 22nd		Employed on improving the Water supply of the area occupied by the division under direction of Water supply officer 1st Army.	
"	16th		2/Lt G.S. HATTON rejoined the unit from the Base.	
WILLENCOURT	22nd		Squadron marched to WILLENCOURT & att'd Cav. Corps for bridging.	
"	23rd – 31st		Squadron training in bridging with Steel boat, Pontoon, Trestle & Inglis (Light Tube) equipments.	
"	26th		Lt Lloyd R.E. proceeded on 14 days leave to England.	

P. Armstrong Major R.E.
O/C. 2nd FIELD SQDN., R.E.

3. R. 18

Confidential

War Diary of
2nd Field Squadron R.E.
From 1.8.18 to 31.8.18

Volume No 48

Army Form C. 2118.

WAR DIARY
or
INTELLIGENCE SUMMARY 2nd FIELD SQUADRON RE

(Erase heading not required.)

Instructions regarding War Diaries and Intelligence Summaries are contained in F. S. Regs., Part II. and the Staff Manual respectively. Title pages will be prepared in manuscript.

[Stamp: 2nd FIELD SQUADRON ROYAL ENGINEERS]

Place	Hour, Date	Summary of Events and Information	Remarks and references to Appendices
AUGUST.			
WILLENCOURT.	1st – 4th.	Squadron Training. Practice bridging with INGLES and Cav. Bridging Equipment.	
HANCHY.	5th/6th.	INGLES + PONTOON bridging Equip'. Sent to 3rd Army Park. 'B' Echelon remained at WILLENCOURT.	
BREILLY.	6th/7th.	Night March to HANCHY. Sqdn. rejoined 2nd Cav. Div.	
LONGEAU.	7th/8th.	" " BREILLY.	
CAIX.	8th.	" " LONGEAU.	
WARVILLERS.	9th.	Moved up to CAIX. bivouaced in W.19.b.	Map. 1/40000 62.D
VRÉLY.	10th.	Moved up to WARVILLERS. bivouaced in Wood. E.23.c	" 1/20000 66.E
"	11th.	" back to CAYEUX. Then up to WARVILLERS and Cough in VRÉLY.	
AUBERCOURT.	11th – 14th.	Euried. Bell raisin Wall retrieden and Gough in VRÉLY. Then dismanified same and went back to AUBERCOURT.	
"	14th.	Started to cross Dt. HQ. now near CAYEUX.	
BELLOY-SUR-SOMME.	15th.	Lt. N.A. CHANCE proceeded to Cav. Corps. Equitation School.	
CANAPLES. (17th).	16th/17th.	Sqdn. marched to BELLOY-SUR-SOMME.	
"	17th/18th.	Night march to CANAPLES.	
CAUMONT.	18th – 21st.	" " CAUMONT. 'B' Echelon rejoined.	
"	21st/22nd.	Sqdn. refitted at CAUMONT.	
GRENAS.	22nd + 23rd.	Night march to GRENAS.	
BAILLEULVAL. (AYETTE).	23rd/24th.	GRENAS.	
BAILLEULVAL.	24th.	Sqdn. marched to BAILLEULVAL. (1 OR injured accidentally + sent to hospital). Then moved up to AYETTE. and reconnoitred water line MOYENNEVILLE - BOYELLES.	
GRENAS.	25th.	" moved back to BAILLEULVAL.	
MIRAUMONT.	26th.	" marched to GRENAS.	
MIRAUMONT.	27th – 31st.	" marched to MIRAUMONT. + Placed under IV Corps Chief Engineer for work.	
		Sqdn. employed under C.E. IV Corps on Horse + General water points at MIRAUMONT.	

31.8.18

J.T. Quennang Major R.E.
OC. 2nd Field Squadron RE.

1247 W 3209 200,000 (E) 8/14 J.B.C. & A. Forms/C. 2116/11.

CONFIDENTIAL
WAR — DIARY
of
2ⁿᵈ FIELD - SQUADRON RE
From 1.9.18 to 30.9.18
Volume - N⁰ 49.

Army Form C. 2118.

WAR DIARY
of 2nd Field Squadron RE

INTELLIGENCE SUMMARY.
(Erase heading not required.)

Instructions regarding War Diaries and Intelligence
Summaries are contained in F. S. Regs., Part II.
and the Staff Manual respectively. Title pages
will be prepared in manuscript.

[Stamp: 2nd FIELD SQUADRON ROYAL ENGINEERS, Date 30/9/18]

Place	Date	Hour	Summary of Events and Information	Remarks and references to Appendices
	SEPTEMBER			
MIRAUMONT	1st–3rd		Squadron Employed under C.E. IX Corps on Water points.	
	3rd		Sqdn. marched to Famechon and rejoined 2nd Cav. Div.	
FAMECHON	3rd–17		" billetted at FAMECHON. experiments carried out with water raising apparatus	
	6th		" attached to Cav. Corps Bridging Park	
	6th		Lt Lloyd's Troop in detached and proceeded to join 5th Bde at ALBERT	
	7th		Lt MacDowall's Troop " " " " 3rd Bde at LATTRE ST QUENTIN	
	8th		No 2 Troop " " with 5th Bde to QUERRIEU	
	10		No 1 Troop " " " 3rd Bde to DIEVAL	
	13th		2 NCO's & 11 men Sent to CAYEUX-SUR-MER to test stations of EQUITATION SCHOOL	
	15.17		Captain WAGHORN RE left to Umpire at Cav. Corps Manoeuvres	
GAUDIEMPRÉ	17th		Squadron moved to GAUDIEMPRÉ	
	17–31		HQrs & 3rd Troop of Squadron billetted at GAUDIEMPRÉ	
	28th		Lt TURNER proceeded to Cav. Corps Equitation School for course	
			No 1 Troop moved with 3rd Bde to WAILLY	
	26th		" 2 Troop " " " 5 Bde to PROYART	
	29th		" 1 Troop " " " 3rd Bde to INCAY-EN-ARTOIS	

S. J. Armstrong
Major RE
OC 2nd Field Squadron RE

Confidential

War Diary of
2nd Field Squadron R.E.
From 1.10.18 to 31.10.18

Volume No. 50

Vol 49

Army Form C. 2118.

WAR DIARY
or
INTELLIGENCE SUMMARY.
(Erase heading not required.)

2nd Field Ambulance

Place	Date	Hour	Summary of Events and Information	Remarks and references to Appendices
CAYEUX	1-31		Major & NO 3 Coy (two detachment 15 mm of CAYEUX) filled QUADIENPRÉ Maps Examining the 4 Capt hospitals left for temporary work under C.R.E. C.E.o IV & V Corps respectively	
	21		St. Aignan, moved from base	
	16		Capt Walker M.C. R.A.M.C. moved from Field Ambulance	
	28		20 Lights taken with 5th Rgt	
	1-31		Remounting party proceeded to link BENOUVOIR - FONSOME line. I.O.R. wounded	
	3		VADENCOURT - MAGNY-LE-FOSSE.	
	6		LEHAUCOURT - MONTBREHAIN	
	7-8		Found BONNIN DOTRON for fire extinguisher & lot of stores and to C.R.E with 9 CRE 6a Div. Trps had been standing by Ragt on several occasions for demolition posts which did not take place owing to enemy opposition Between a demonstration to Ragt on demolition	
	10		It likely to enable brigade or night match cross creation from to St Souplet trps attached 3rd Rgt	
	1-31			Malum Lt RE att 5th CN & 9th CN

CONFIDENTIAL

War Diary

November 1918 Volume No 51

Army Form C. 2118.

WAR DIARY

INTELLIGENCE SUMMARY. 2nd Field Squadron R.E.

(Erase heading not required.)

Instructions regarding War Diaries and Intelligence
Summaries are contained in F. S. Regs., Part II
and the Staff Manual respectively. Title pages
will be prepared in manuscript.

Place	Date	Hour	Summary of Events and Information	Remarks and references to Appendices
NOVEMBER				
QUAD.15M.PRÉ	1st-5th		H.Q. and 3rd Troop of Field Squadron billeted at QUADISMPRÉ under LT CHANCE. No.1 Troop LT. MACDOWELL att'd 3rd Cav. Bde. & No.2 Troop LT LLOYD att'd 5th Cav. Bde.	
BAPAUME	5th		Sqdn. marched to area near BAPAUME.	
CAMBRAI	6th		" " " CAMBRAI and quartered in Cavalry Barracks. Major ARMSTRONG rejoined Squadron	
"	5th		from 4th Corps and Resumed Command. Capt. WAGHORN att'd C.E. 5th Corps was temporarily att'd to 1st F'd Sqdn as 2nd in Command.	
"	6th-13th		Sqdn. quartered at CAMBRAI	
"	12th		LT FOX. J.N. R.E. joined the Squadron from the base.	
"	"		LT TURNER rejoined with 12 Sappers from the equitation School (Cav Corps) at CAYEUX, where they had been employed on building stables. LT TURNER had attended equitation course.	
BOUSIES	13th		Sqdn. marched to BOUSIES.	
HUGEMONT CHAT	14th		" " " HUGEMONT CHAT near TAISNIÈRES	
MAUBEUGE	15th		" " " MAUBEUGE	
"	16th		No.3 Troop under LT CHANCE proceeded to join 4th Cav. Bdg. at BOUSSOIS. Capt WAGHORN rejoined Sqdn from 1st Field Sqdn. LT TURNER joined No.1 Troop with 3rd Cav. Bde.	
LOBBES	17th		H.Q. F'd Sqdn marched to LOBBES. Troops employed under Bdes. in removing charges and mines.	
HANZINELLE	18th		" " " HANZINELLE.	
"	"		LT HATTON proceed from No.2 Troop to CAYEUX to take equitation course.	
"	18th-21st		H.Q. and Sqdn billeted at HANZINELLE cleaning up.	
DINANT	21st		" " " marched to DINANT.	
CHAPOIS	22nd		" " " CHAPOIS near LEIGNON	
JAMOGNE	23rd		" " " JAMOGNE MARCHE. LT CHANCE evacuated to Hospital Sick	
"	23rd-29th		" " " billeted at JAMOGNE	

Page II.
Army Form C. 2118.

WAR DIARY
INTELLIGENCE SUMMARY 2nd Field Squadron, R.E.

(Erase heading not required.)

Place	Date	Hour	Summary of Events and Information	Remarks and references to Appendices
JAMODINE	November 29th		H.Q, F'd Sqdn. marched to MARLOIE and hds 1 & 3 Troops attached 15 3rd & 4th Can. Bdes rejoined 15 Sqdn. at MARLOIE	
MARLOIE	29th & 30th		F'd Sqdn. at MARLOIE less 2nd Troop. Lt. LLOYD.R.E still att O/c 5 Can. Bde during the advance of New Bde. into GERMANY. Lt. A.H.LLOYD R.E awarded a bar to his M.C. for bravery and devotion to duty at RONAIN, with 5th Can.Bde. when he rendered safe several mines and successfully put out the fire the Germans had lit at the PIONEER PARK	
	30.11.18			

J.F. Armstrong
Major R.E.
O/c. 2nd FIELD SQDN., R.E.

Nr. 51 R 358
1.1.1918

Kriegstagebuch
War — Diary
of
2ᵐ Feldart. Schwadron R8.
Volume No 62.
From 1.12.18 to 31.12.18

Army Form C. 2118.

WAR DIARY
or
INTELLIGENCE SUMMARY.
(Erase heading not required.)

2nd Field Squadron – R.E.

Place	Date	Hour	Summary of Events and Information	Remarks and references to Appendices
DECEMBER				
MAREDIE	1st–15th		Field Squadron billetted at MAREDIE. Minor Engineer Services. Reconnaissance of Bridges etc. given to 2 Troop. (Lt LLOYD) still with 5th Cav. Bde.	
	16th		Squadron marched to 12 IEA.	
TILFF	17th		Squadron marched to TILFF	
"	20th		No 2 Troop. (Lt LLOYD.) rejoined Squadron at TILFF	
"	17th–31st		Squadron remained at TILFF employed on minor Engineer Services and Reconnaissance of Bridges and Sites in the Divisional Area.	
	9th		Interpreter VANNES (Mauricene de Logie) att.d this unit will be awarded the MERITORIOUS SERVICE MEDAL.	

J.T. Quinnen
Major R.E.
O.C. 2nd Field Squadron, R.E.

Confidential War Diary
of
2nd Field Squadron R.E.
From 1.1.19 to 31.1.19
Volume No 53.

Vol 52

Army Form C. 2118.

WAR DIARY
—of—
INTELLIGENCE SUMMARY.
(Erase heading not required.)

Place	Date	Hour	Summary of Events and Information	Remarks and references to Appendices
TILFF	January		Squadron at TILFF	
	1st to 5th			
	6th		Lieut Lerner RE rejoined from leave	
	6 & 7		Work on baths at CHAUDEFONTAINE	
	8th		C.R.E. proceeds on leave.	
	9th to 12th		Minor RE duties & education.	
	13th		T/2nd Lieut F.R. EVERSHED RE to T/Lieut H. METLING RE joined from Base.	
	15th		Interpreter VANNES (Mon-cli- rosin) left unit.	
	16th 17th		Minor RE duties	
	18th		M.T. Course of Instruction commenced. Major S.J. ARMSTRONG M.C. R.E. left for England on leave to then to join up at CHATHAM for course on 31st January.	
	19th		Inspection and classification of horses by veterinary branch	
	20th		14 ORs left for demobilization	
	21st		Half REPRS commenced at VERVIERS under orders of 2nd Army. Inspection & classification of horses by Remount Board. 7 ORs left for demobilization.	
	22nd		Minor RE duties	
	23rd		25883 E.C. Sergt S.G. COOK. & 7562 Cpl. T. TINGEY — awarded M.S.M.	

Army Form C. 2118.

WAR DIARY
INTELLIGENCE SUMMARY.
(Erase heading not required.)

Instructions regarding War Diaries and Intelligence Summaries are contained in F.S. Regs., Part II. and the Staff Manual respectively. Title pages will be prepared in manuscript.

Place	Date	Hour	Summary of Events and Information	Remarks and references to Appendices
11LFF	23rd		Congratulating Cards from Divisional Commander awarded to :- 11167 Sapper H. GALE. 24813 L.Cpl A.JACKSON - 20302 Cpl E.WILSON. 22230 Sapper W. URE. 26232 Sapper E. ARKELL - 121323 L.Cpl A. HAWKINS - 24067 - DRIVER T. TRAYNOR - 139932 Sapper W. FLINT 16749 - Sapper L. GODDEN - 25931 Sapper E.G. MILLER - 26040 Sapper W.J. BROWN - 34983 Sapper F.H. Tonge - 120882 Sapper J. GIBSON (All for gallant conduct & devotion to duty.)	
	23rd		2nd Lieut C.E.F. TURNER left for course at R.E. Field Survey Battalion G.H.Q	
	24th		Horses malienes	
	25th 31st		Minor R.E. duties. Lieut Mac Dowell returned from leave 25th inst	

W.Brighton Capt RE
OC 2nd Army Section

1. 2. 19.

Army Form C. 2118.

WAR DIARY
or
INTELLIGENCE SUMMARY.
(Erase heading not required.)

Jan. 1919   2nd Signal Squadron R.E.

Instructions regarding War Diaries and Intelligence Summaries are contained in F. S. Regs., Part II. and the Staff Manual respectively. Title pages will be prepared in manuscript.

Place	Date JAN.	Hour	Summary of Events and Information	Remarks and references to Appendices
THEUX	1 to 8		Nothing to report	
THEUX	9th to 16th		Lt H. Braid. demobilised. Lt Lord A.F. Hill took over squadron temporarily. 13.1.19.	
THEUX	17th 18th 19th 20th 21st 22nd 23rd 24th 25th 26th		Nothing to report	
			Capt. A.C. Hardinge arrived from England and took over command of the Squadron from Lt Lord A.F. Hill. Lt Lord A.F. Hill returned to 5th Cav Bde HQ.	
	27th 28th 29th 30th 31st		Nothing to report.	

A.C. Hardinge Capt
for 2nd Sig Sqdn R.E.

Vol 52

2nd Field Squadron I.E.

War Diary

Volume No. 54.

From 1.2.19 to 28.2.19

Army Form C. 2118.

WAR DIARY
or
INTELLIGENCE SUMMARY.
(Erase heading not required.)

Instructions regarding War Diaries and Intelligence Summaries are contained in F. S. Regs., Part II. and the Staff Manual respectively. Title pages will be prepared in manuscript.

Place	Date	Hour	Summary of Events and Information	Remarks and references to Appendices
TILFF	FEBRUARY			
	1st		Bested RE left Spda on being demobilized.	
	2nd–8th		Minor RE reliefs	
	9th		Lt. K.M. Macdowell RE — — — — —	
	13–14		Pd. of J hours to Belg. civilians	
			Minor Reliefs	
	16th		Capt. FOX JAN M.C. RE went to last Corps to take over from	
			Capt. Gardner as adj. CRE Can Corps.	
	17th		A.D.R. out to SERAING got lorries or P.O.W. camp which Can Corps	
	20th		SPDA for work in recovering cable & to Bde	
			8 OR — — returned	
	22nd		A.D.R. returned	
			Collection of German materiel began	
	24th		Capt R.S. Boyton RE left for duty & leave	
	26th		Capt Walker M.O. (RAMC) left for duty as ADMS.	
	27th 28th		All German material now collected at MERY.	

DEMOBILIZATION

A.M. Lloyd Lt. Col. R.E. for O.C. 2nd Hsy Sr.

CONFIDENTIAL WAR DIARY

2ND FIELD SQUADRON R.E.

VOLUME No 55   MARCH 1919

Army Form C. 2118.

WAR DIARY
or
INTELLIGENCE SUMMARY.
(Erase heading not required.)

Instructions regarding War Diaries and Intelligence Summaries are contained in F.S. Regs., Part II. and the Staff Manual respectively. Title pages will be prepared in manuscript.

Place	Date	Hour	Summary of Events and Information	Remarks and references to Appendices
TILFF	March 1-8th		Minor R.E. duties. Work on racecourse at SPA.	
	9th		Squadron ordered to relieve 1st CADRE A.	
	10th		------- Come up to --- B.	
ENSIVAL	12-16th		Squadron marches to ENSIVAL preparatory to returning to England. Minor R.E. duties.	
	16-18th		Work on racecourse at FAYS under 5th Cav. Bde.	
	19th		Made up work & horse for CADRE B. 135. Capt. A.B. Ingham R.E. returns from Leave.	
	19-31st		Minor R.E. duties. Order received for (A/Capt.) R.S. Ingham R.E. & Lt. A.H. Lloyd, M.C. R.E. to go on report to 1st Flt.Sqdn R.E. for duty with Army of Occupation. 30th Capt. J.N. Fox M.C. R.E. struck off Strength of Lines from 24.2.19. On being A.M.S. Cavly Corps R. 321/432 .B	

R.W. Ingham C/Mr.
Br. 2nd Field Squadron R.E.

31.3.19.

2ND FIELD SQUADRON RE
CONFIDENTIAL.

WAR DIARY

VOLUME - Nº 58 APRIL, 1919.

WAR DIARY
or
INTELLIGENCE SUMMARY.

(Erase heading not required.)

Army Form C. 2118.

Place	Date	Hour	Summary of Events and Information	Remarks and references to Appendices
ENSIVAL	April 12th		Lt C Shebwry RE arrived from 1st Field Squad RE	
	13th		Lt C Shebwry RE took over 2nd Field Sqdn RE Section from Capt Ethinghorn RE	
	14th		Capt RA Nayhan left ENSIVAL to join 3rd Field Sqdn RE A.P.O.	
	15th		O.R's despatched to Concentts for demand ? "	
	23rd		O.R's despatched to Concentts for demand ? "	
	24th		O.R's despatched to Concentts for demand ? "	
	30th		Strength of Cadre -- 1 Off. 39 O.R's	

C Shebwry/Lt RE.
O.C. 2nd Field Squadron RE

www.ingramcontent.com/pod-product-compliance
Lightning Source LLC
Chambersburg PA
CBHW081537160426
43191CB00011B/1780